CURIOSITIES
— OF —
CRICKET

JONATHAN RICE

with cartoons by
Robert Duncan

PAVILION

First published in Great Britain in 1993 by
PAVILION BOOKS LIMITED
26 Upper Ground, London SE1 9PD

Text copyright © Jonathan Rice 1993
Cartoons copyright © Robert Duncan 1993
Title page illustration © Peter Cross 1993

Designed by Nigel Partridge

A CIP catalogue record for this book is available from the British
Library

Hardback ISBN 1 85145 929 4
Paperback ISBN 1 85793 270 6

Printed and bound in Great Britain by
Butler & Tanner Ltd, Frome and London

2 4 6 8 10 9 7 5 3 1

The author and publisher are grateful for permission to use extracts
from these works: *The Gay Sussex Cricketers* by
Gerard Durani Martineau reproduced by kind permission of
The Cricketer Limited; and *Sprigs of Nobility We* from
Batter Suite or Not Cricket by Vivian Ellis

This book may be ordered by post direct from the publisher
Please contact the Marketing Department
But try your bookshop first

CONTENTS

INTRODUCTION

Mary Turner, in a letter to a friend from her home in East Hoathly, Sussex, on 'September 2th' 1739, writes, 'Last Mundaye youre Father was at Mr Payn's and plaid Cricket, and came home please enuf for he struck the best ball in the Game and whishd he had not annything else to do he ould play at Cricket all his Life.'

Two hundred and fifty years later, there are still plenty of us who wish we 'had not annything else to do', because then we too would play at cricket all our lives. But failing that, we can at least rejoice in the way that cricket mirrors life and life reflects cricket, so that to live every day is to play cricket all our lives. It was one of the few Prime Ministers of England with no interest in cricket and little sense of humour who remarked, as she left office, 'It's a funny old world'. Had she turned to the sports pages before the parliamentary reports in her newspaper every morning, perhaps even she would have discovered that the world is just as funny on the cricket field as off it. This book is an attempt to prove it, in both the peculiar and the ha-ha sense.

The original *Curiosities of Cricket* was published privately in 1897 by D. B. Friend & Co. of Brighton. Its full title was 'Curiosities Of Cricket from The Earliest Records to The Present Time, by An Old Cricketer'. The Old Cricketer in question was one Alfred Lawson Ford, who was actually just 53 years old when he had a modest 25 copies of his booklet printed. Ford played for Southgate CC for many years, and held the proud record, a curiosity in itself, that between 1860, when he left school, and 1904 he bowled in every match in which he took part. He was the compiler of the *Index to Scores and Biographies, Volumes I to XIII*, which were the basis of many of his abstruse and learned entries in his *Curiosities of Cricket*. He was also one of the first great collectors of cricketana. He died in 1924.

Ford's work was one long and often very funny list, comprising items ranging from 'Balls hit into linnet's nest' to 'Batsman walking round wicket between time of bowler starting to deliver ball and its delivery', which is a peculiar habit that one Lieut. Leucadore showed when playing for the Phoenix Club against Carlow in the 1890s. He also lists instances of teams all out for 0, tied matches and batting averages of 82, which are more commonplace now, as are events such as 'Toe of batsman broken in hitting at ball' and 'Wides bowled to put batsman out of temper'.

I have not attempted to duplicate the style or methods of An Old Cricketer in unearthing some of the more bizarre happenings connected however slightly with cricket. There are some lists, where there is no room to expand on the bare bones of the curiosity in question, but where possible I have given the full context of the event. All the curiosities are items that have been reported in cricket literature over the past century and more, and provided we can trust the honesty of the original recorder of the event, they are all true. I have not tried to list all the cases of, for example, matches played in snow, or dogs who have stopped play. I am sure there are many others, which only goes to prove that curiosities are not as curious as they used to be.

I have had a great deal of help from all sorts of people, who have told me anecdotes or pointed out statistical oddities that I might otherwise have missed. In particular, I would like to thank David Bromage, Ken Lewsey, Chester McKaige, my brother Tim Rice and Barry Uden for their daft contributions to this book. My son Alex has been my main right-hand man, having researched diligently through piles of old magazines and newspapers to come up with many curious stories, often involving stoats, for which I am suitably grateful. Any mistakes are, of course, mine alone.

JONATHAN RICE
September 1992

A CHAPTER OF █ ACCIDENTS

Accidents are a part of life. On the cricket field, the malign hand of fate seems to follow the innocent to such an extent that many types of accident can no longer be described as curiosities. A broken finger is not a curiosity, as most people who play regularly have broken a finger at one time or another. This chapter is being typed with one finger fewer than usual for precisely this reason: a sharp chance in the slips taken on the half volley reducing the number of workable fingers on my right hand to three and a thumb. Time and editorial deadlines wait for no man, not even a wounded second slip. Like all good cricketers, I am able to disguise my ever slowing reactions and my incompetence in the field under a large bandage and the phrase 'a sharp chance in the slips taken on the half volley'. This is no accident, of course. It is an untruth. I not only dropped an easy catch, I broke my finger as well. It was no sharp chance, not even a half volley. It went in and out of my hands via the topmost joint of the third finger of my right hand. My team-mates looked upon the event with mixed emotions. The bad news was that the catch had gone to ground. The good news was that, with me off in the first aid tent, somebody who knew how to field could be brought on in my place.

A simple broken finger is not a curiosity, but three consecutive broken fingers on the left hand, each broken in the first match of three consecutive seasons, certainly is. This happened to Andy Rice, a schoolboy at Lancing College, in the seasons of 1963, 1964 and 1965. He never made it to the First XI.

A finger broken by a ball off which the batsman was given 'not out' caught behind is also a curiosity. This is reputed to have happened in a Test match between West Indies and Pakistan, and the batsman retired hurt at the end of the over, unable to carry on, but still, in defiance of both the Laws and the opposition, not out. Test matches between West Indies and Pakistan have produced a depressing number of 'accidents' involving the spectators. Courtney Walsh and Sylvester Clarke of West Indies have been at either end of missile-throwing incidents with Pakistan spectators, and Abdul Qadir became involved in a flurry of punches with a West Indian spectator during the Third Test at Bridgetown, Barbados, on 27 April 1988.

9

If finger breakages are commonplace, there is at least one instance of a batsman having his leg broken by a fast delivery. The Rev. Walter Marcon (1824–1875), an Old Etonian, was one of the fastest of all bowlers in the 1840s. At Oxford, he broke the leg of a batsman, and was reputed to need three longstops behind the wicketkeeper. This was at a time when boundaries were rarely marked, and the bowling was all underarm. Wickets were less well kept in those days, which may explain the viciousness of the Rev. Marcon's bowling. It was said that the only way the wicket resembled a billiard table was that both had pockets.

Death while playing is unfortunately not rare. Perhaps because village cricketers refuse to admit the passage of time, many elderly players have died at the wicket, usually from a heart attack. Andrew Ducat, the Arsenal, Aston Villa and England soccer international and Surrey and England cricketer, collapsed and died, aged 56, while batting at Lord's on 23 July 1942, playing for the Surrey Home Guard against Sussex Home Guard. The match was abandoned, and Ducat's score was entered in the scorebook as 'not out 29'. Quite the best way to die.

Deaths at Lord's have not been limited to the players, of course. Members are occasionally found to have died while watching the game from the splendour of the pavilion. During the Gillette Cup Final of 1975 or 1976, a member was found dead in his seat at six o'clock in the evening, with an almost full glass of beer locked between his by now quite stiff knees. By checking with the barman who served him his final pint, it was possible

to pinpoint the time of death at shortly after twelve noon.

During a Lord's Test in the early 1980s, a member was found to have died in his seat on one of the balconies in the pavilion. It was just after tea, and rather than alarm the rest of the members on one of the busiest days of the Lord's year, a member of the ground staff was deputed to sit next to the corpse, and talk to him until close of play, so that none of the other spectators would realize he was dead. After stumps had been drawn and the pavilion emptied, the late member was removed to his final resting-place.

Perhaps the most famous spectator death was at the Oval Test of 1882. This was the match which Australia won by seven runs and which prompted the mock obituary in the *Sporting Times*: 'In Affectionate Remembrance of ENGLISH CRICKET which died at the Oval on 29th August 1882. Deeply lamented by a large circle of Sorrowing Friends and Acquaintances. R.I.P. N.B. – The body will be cremated, and the Ashes taken to Australia.' One English spectator chewed right through the handle of his umbrella, and another dropped dead in the excitement of the closing moments. The name of this unfortunate person is not recorded in any contemporary report, and it is possible that the dead man may have been entirely apochryphal, invented to add intensity to memories of a long past excitement.

The only first-class cricket match to have been brought to a premature close because of the death of a woman was Lancashire v Gloucestershire on 25 July 1884. The lady who died was Mrs Martha Grace, mother of two of the Gloucestershire players in that match, Dr W. G. Grace and his elder brother Dr E. M. Grace. Mrs Grace remains the only woman to feature in *Wisden*'s 'Births and Deaths of Cricketers'.

Cricket has even caused the death of someone who was not even a spectator at the time. In 1987, it was reported that cricket had been banned from the streets of Srinagar and other towns in the Kashmir, after a scooter rider was killed by a cricket ball.

There have been many cricketers who have died in wartime, from Colin Blythe, Tibby Cotter and Percy Jeeves in the First World War, to Kenneth Farnes, Hedley Verity and Maurice Turnbull in the Second World War, as well as thousands of less famous names. But the first international cricketer to die in wartime was an American. Captain Walter Symonds Newhall of the 3rd Pennsylvanian Cavalry played for the United States against Canada at Toronto in 1859 and at Hoboken, New Jersey (later the birthplace of Frank Sinatra), in 1860. He also played against George Parr's English tourists in October

1859. He was a Union officer in the American Civil War, and drowned in the Rappahannock River in Virginia on 18 December 1863, aged only 22.

Perhaps the only soldier to have been killed by enemy action while actually playing cricket was Corporal Harris, who was playing for an Army cricket team against the police at Folkestone in August 1942, when a Focke Wulf 190 fighter bomber flew over the ground. Harris, fielding at mid-on, was going for the ball when a bomb exploded a short distance from the pitch, and he was killed. Lieutenant G. Wood, who was bowling, was also injured. He was thrown into the air by the blast of the bomb, but escaped with a sprained ankle. The Chief Constable was pinned to the ground by debris, but otherwise unhurt.

Gordon Rudolph Piper, aged 23, an Australian lodging in Coleswood Road, Harpenden, committed suicide in 1930 because England won the first Test of that year's series. Having cut his throat and summoned a doctor, he then dictated his will to a fellow lodger, who wrote it down, and Piper signed it. He died a little later in St Albans Infirmary. This was undoubtedly a misguided act, because Australia went on to win the series 2–1, with Donald Bradman scoring 974 runs at an average of 139.14, to regain the Ashes lost in 1926.

Less fatal injuries have been picked up in the most unlikely circumstances. Derek Pringle had to miss a Test match after injuring his back while writing a letter. Jeff Thomson, the Australian fast bowler, injured himself playing tennis on 28 January 1975, the rest day of the Fifth Test against England, and had to miss the rest of

13

that match and the final Test, which England won. Ted Dexter broke his leg when his own car ran him over, and Gil Langley, the Australian wicketkeeper of the 1950s, once missed a Test because he injured a hand by lying on it while sleeping. A. Dolphin of Yorkshire broke his wrist in 1921 falling off a chair while reaching for his clothes in the Yorkshire dressing-room at Lord's. The following year, S. L. Amor, the Somerset wicketkeeper, broke his wrist when his car backfired as he turned the starting handle. In 1989, Essex bowler Don Topley had to miss his county's pre-season practice matches after hurting his hand on a spring-loaded letterbox while delivering a letter to a friend.

14

Ian Greig, of Cambridge University, Sussex and Surrey, broke his right ankle on 8 June 1983 after the first day's play in the Sussex v. Kent county match, during which he scored 42. He fell 18 feet trying to climb into his flat after his key had broken in the lock. Four years later, on 3 May 1987, in only his third match as captain of Surrey, Greig was hit on the finger while batting against the Pakistan tourists. He was out after scoring only 5, and that evening went to the hospital to have his finger X-rayed. A fracture was confirmed, and as Greig rose to leave, he cracked his head on the X-ray machine. He required two stitches. Given his proneness to injury, it is perhaps not surprising that the entry under I. A. Greig in Derek Barnard's authoritative *Index to Wisden 1864–1984* merely reads 'Obituary 1982, page 573'.

When Steven Rhodes was playing for The York-shiremen against Yorkshire at Scarborough on 6 September 1990, he hit five sixes in his first 50 runs, which took 29 minutes. It would have been even quicker except that one of his sixes struck a spectator standing by the pavilion. The unfortunate spectator was dusted down, but seen to be largely unharmed, and played continued. Five minutes later Rhodes hit another six, striking the same spectator again. One of the players then came off the field to offer him a helmet.

Practising can be as dangerous as playing or watching cricket. Martyn Goulding, of Torquay, was taking net practice in the winter of 1985–86, batting against a bowling machine. A 75 mph delivery hit his foot, breaking a bone. As he lay on the ground writhing in agony, the pitiless machine bowled its next delivery, which hit the unfortunate Mr Goulding again, breaking two of his ribs.

John Edrich once sprained his ankle treading on the ball during a pre-match fielding practice session, causing him to miss a couple of games, and there is the terrible case of the Gloucestershire opener in the 1960s who trod on his own hand while walking down the pavilion steps

15

before play began. Bruce French, as accident-prone as any wicketkeeper of recent years, required four stitches after a net practice in Lahore on 12 November 1987. He was hit over the left eye by a poor return from a spectator. On arrival at the hospital, a car hit him (rather slowly, it must be admitted) on the leg, and after the stitching had been completed, he hit his head on a light fitting as he rose to leave.

16   On the field of play, injuries can take the most extreme form. Two players died from stab wounds after a church fund-raising cricket match between the villages of Falevau and Sauano, in Western Samoa, in 1977. Six men were arrested. Farhan Shahzada, a Lahore student, died in 1987 after being hit in the neck by a stray bullet fired during victory celebrations after a match at the Punjab University ground.

Fielders were always in danger when C. I. 'Buns' Thornton was at the wicket. Thornton (1850–1929), who played for Cambridge University, Kent and Middlesex and founded the Scarborough Cricket Festival, was a mighty hitter, and in 1922 he recorded an incident at Malton, Yorkshire when Malton were playing Scarborough. 'There was a pond in one corner of the ground, and E. S. Carter put a man beyond the pond to catch me out. I hit one just right; the fieldsman forgot the pond and went clean into it. It was shallow, so no harm resulted.' When playing for the United North against Bingley and District, Thornton hit one hard and high which cover point chased backwards as the ball soared over his head. He was not looking where he was going, and the inevitable happened. He fell into a river, but as the sympathetic Thornton records, 'it was fortunately low at the time'. Non-swimmers were never safe playing against Thornton.

Michael Mates MP, the man who masterminded the challenge of Michael Heseltine for the leadership of the Conservative Party, and thus the downfall of Mrs Thatcher, is one of the few cricketers to have had his jaw broken by a policeman. The act was not a political statement but a pure cricketing accident. While playing for the Lords and Commons against the West Indian Wanderers in 1978, Mates was felled by PC Brian Mustill, playing for the opposition, and was thus rendered speechless for several days. Many other Members of Parliament have since been urged to take up cricket, especially against the West Indian Wanderers, but without the same satisfying results.

The need for a helmet has never been more clearly demonstrated than by David Pritchard, who was playing in a charity match on a windy day in 1988. He was knocked out when the figure '0' blew off the scoreboard and hit him on the head as he was walking out to bat. The accepted practice in major games is for the new batsman to walk to the crease carrying his helmet, so that the crowd can see who it is coming out to bat, but in the light of Mr Pritchard's accident perhaps the TCCB should rethink.

One of the most wholesale cases of injury occurred during the Fourth Test between West Indies and India at Kingston, Jamaica, in April 1976. On the last day of that match, 25 April, India completed their second innings with five men absent injured. In the first innings Viswanath had been dismissed by a ball from Holding that fractured and dislocated his finger; Gaekwad retired hurt after being struck on the left ear, and Patel had three stitches inserted after receiving a blow to his mouth. Bedi, the Indian captain, declared their first innings closed in protest against the intimidatory bowling, and in the second innings, he and Chandrasekhar were also listed as 'absent hurt'. 'Absent so as not to be hurt' might have been more appropriate. The Indian second innings totalled only 97, of which Mohinder Amarnath made a brilliant 60. During this match, all 17 members of the Indian touring party fielded. Surinder Amarnath, Mohinder's elder brother, who fielded as substitute for much of West Indies' first innings, was rushed to hospital on the fourth day with appendicitis, so a substitute for the substitute had to be found.

Only one Test match opening batsman has ever gone through his entire Test career without being dismissed. This is Andy Lloyd, of Warwickshire, whose only match for England was the First Test against West Indies at Edgbaston, his home ground, in 1984. After seven overs, with his score on 10, Lloyd was hit on the side of the head by a ball from Malcolm Marshall. He spent five days in hospital, was out of first-class cricket for the rest of the season, and has never played Test cricket since.

Some Test cricketers have continued playing despite major injuries. Malcolm Marshall himself broke his left thumb in two places on the first morning of the Third

Test of that series, fielding a shot from Chris Broad. He returned to the fray, heavily plastered, and not only scored four runs batting at No. 11, but also took 7 for 53 in England's second innings. The England batsmen complained that his bright white plaster was a distraction as Marshall ran up to bowl, but the real reason for his success was that he was too good. In the next Test, Paul Terry finished his Test career in plaster after a ball from Winston Davis broke his left arm. He returned at the end of the innings to bat on, but owing to some confusion over whether he was there to help Allan Lamb reach a Test century or to try to prevent the follow-on, he found himself taking strike against Joel Garner, and lasted only two more balls. Lamb got his hundred, but England failed to save the follow-on, and were eventually defeated by an innings and 64 runs.

Colin Cowdrey also came out to bat with his arm in plaster, at the very end of the Lord's Test against West Indies in 1963. In this case, however, he did not have to face either of the two balls remaining, against which David Allen defended carefully, and England earned a draw in one of the tightest finishes ever seen in a Test at Lord's.

The motor car has played a significant part in the recent history of cricket. The Northampton v. West Indies match at Northampton in June 1976 was suspended for precisely 37 minutes when a motor car went out of control. One youth sustained a broken leg, and the elderly driver was treated for shock. Play was abandoned in the final of a six-a-side festival at Beaconsfield Cricket Club in July 1992 after a car ran across the pitch, and injured four spectators. The car was being driven by the president of Beaconsfield CC, 86-year-old Mr Tom Orford, who had come to present the prizes.

20

OVERTHROWS

Backside sprained playing cricket
William Byrd, Williamsburg, Virginia, 1710

Batsmen retiring because of sawdust in the eye
Capt. T. O. Jameson (MCC), Lord's, May 1921

Batsman run down by motorized luggage trolley
Trevor Franklin (NZ), Gatwick Airport, Sept 1986

Contact lenses swallowed by wicketkeeper
Steve Marsh (Kent) swallowed Graham Cowdrey's lenses, May 1988

Death of batsman struck on head by ball from J. Platts
George Summers (Notts), MCC v. Nottinghamshire, Lord's, 1870

Death of batsman struck over heart by ball
Abdul Aziz, aged 17 (Karachi), Karachi v. Services, 1959

Death of fielder from blow on head while attempting catch
W. Jupp, Gorton, 1891

Death of fielder from falling over cliff when following ball
St Helena, 1886

Death of man falling from flag-staff while affixing county flag
Brown, Trent Bridge, 1879

Finger broken by last ball ever received in first-class cricket
C. E. Dench (Notts) by W. R. Cuttell (Lancs), Trent Bridge,
1902

First-class cricketers killed in motor accidents include
George Street (Sussex), 24 Apr 1924
D. F. Pope (Glos and Essex), 8 Sep 1934
Reginald Northway (Somerset and Northants), 26 Aug 1936
D. A. C. Page (Glos), 2 Sep 1936
William Carkeek (Victoria and Australia), 21 Feb 1937
Ted McDonald (Tasmania, Victoria, Lancs and Australia), 22
July 1937
Charles Bull (Kent and Worcs), 28 May 1939
G. V. Gunn (Notts), 15 Oct 1957
Brian Swift (Oxford U.), 8 Mar 1958
O. G. 'Collie' Smith (Jamaica and West Indies), 9 Sep 1959
Harry Crick (Yorks), 10 Feb 1960
Vic Jackson (New South Wales and Leics), 30 Jan 1965
Dr R. H. B. Bettington (Oxford U., Middx, and New South
Wales), 24 Jun 1969

First-class cricketers with only one good eye
William Clarke (Notts)
W. H. Fryer (Kent)
John Kinloch (New South Wales) wore a monocle
James Lillywhite Snr
Mansur Ali Khan, Nawab of Pataudi Jnr (Oxford U. and
India)
C. Milburn (Northants and England)
E. P. Nupen (Transvaal and South Africa)
J. W. Sharpe (Surrey)

Four toes lost in motor boat accident
F. J. Titmus (Middx and England), in West Indies, Feb 1968

Given out lbw to a ball that broke his jaw in two places
C. T. M. Pugh, Gloucestershire v. Northamptonshire,
Northampton, 17 May 1961

Groin muscle torn lifting heavy suitcase
Mohammed Azharuddin (India), Perth, Dec 1991

Loss of eye by running on to an iron used to identify pitches on a ground where as many as 100 pitches were in use
Giles, a fieldsman, London, 1903

Opposing wicketkeepers dying on same day
H. Crick (Yorks) and E. W. J. Brooks (Surrey), wicketkeepers in Yorkshire v. Surrey match in 1937, both died on 10 Feb 1960

Player requiring 5 stitches in hand after accident with champagne bottle
Ian Botham (Somerset), Jun 1984

Prime Minister top edges ball into glasses
Bob Hawke (Aus), Parliament v. Press, Canberra, Nov 1984

Retired with measles on 99 not out
G. E. V. Crutchley, Oxford v. Cambridge, 8 Jul 1912

Selected for Northamptonshire despite losing part of leg in Great War
A. D. Denton, Northamptonshire v. Leicestershire, Northampton, Jun 1919

Shot in leg by air-gun pellet while fielding on the boundary
John Holden, Linden Park v. Leigh, 10 Jul 1989

Spectators killed by lightning
Norman Elliott and Miss Alice Dumma, Jedburgh, 26 Aug 1939

Umpire's ankle injured by straight drive
H. D. 'Dickie' Bird, by Graham Gooch off Bob Holland, England v. Australia, 1985

Umpire's neck broken by straight drive
Jeremy Daykin, Long Eaton v. Nottinghamshire Amateurs, 31 May 1986

BATTING TO
REMEMBER

Cricket is a game for batsmen. Never mind that it is the bowler who starts the game off, or that the fielders, throwing themselves after the ball, bringing off famous catches or stopping certain fours, give spectators as much delight as any square cut or cultured off drive. The Laws of Cricket were framed for the batsman, the glories of cricket are reserved for the batsman, and the most famous names in cricket history are almost all those of batsmen. Batting, that curious sideways art of striking a ball, is the hub of cricket. Not everybody is given the chance to bowl, and all too many show that they have no talent or enthusiasm for fielding, but every cricketer has a go at batting. Some cricketers even make a legal point of not bowling. Tom Hayward, the Surrey and England professional who was Jack Hobbs's first cricketing hero, began life as an all-rounder. He took 481 wickets during his first-class career, including two hat-tricks in 1899, and achieved the double in 1897, but he found bowling to be too much like hard work for his taste. In his later years with Surrey, up to the beginning of the Great War, he had a clause in his contracts of employment with the county which stipulated that he would not be asked to bowl in any of the county's matches. As his fellow Surrey professional of a later era, Alec Bedser, once remarked, 'The last bowler to be knighted was Sir Francis Drake'. Since then, of course, both Sir George Allen and Sir Richard Hadlee have felt the sword on the shoulder, but the fact remains: cricket is a game for batsmen.

It is not surprising, then, that the title of Worst Batsman in the World is one that is highly sought-after. The candidates for the title are many. In 1992, Devon Malcolm was described by the ICC Test match referee Conrad Hunte as 'perhaps the worst No. 11 in Test cricket', but this is still pretty high up the batting ranking. For Derbyshire that season, Malcolm was the regular No. 10, which makes Ole Mortensen, at No. 11, theoretically even worse. Fred Morley, the Nottinghamshire bowler of the 1870s, was pretty awful too. 'When Morley used to go in to bat at Trent Bridge, the aged horse used to meander out of the shed on its own initiative, and wander up to the roller, ready for the groundsman', according to *The Cricketer* magazine in 1922. Eric Hollies, of Warwickshire

and England, the man who bowled Donald Bradman for 0 in his final Test innings, was one of the few players who took more wickets than he scored runs in his career. For his county, he scored only 1,544 runs at an average of 4.95, but took 2,201 wickets. The world record for consecutive innings without scoring in first-class cricket was set by Northamptonshire's Mark Robinson in 1990. The first three innings of his season brought him scores of 1*, 0* and 1, but from 4 May until 13 September that year, he failed to score in 12 consecutive innings, of which seven were not out. He rounded off his year with 1 not out against Leicestershire, thus ending his season with three runs at an average of 0.50. He took 38 wickets in the season, so by taking 12.67 times as many wickets as he scored runs, he established a first-class record. In 1991, he returned to his native Yorkshire, and scored as many as 17 runs in the season, while taking only 23 wickets. To the end of 1992, in the first six seasons of his career, he had scored 120 runs at 2.30, but taken 226 wickets.

Robinson is a Yorkshireman. Despite Yorkshire's proud boast that it has raised some of the greatest batsmen in the world, from Herbert Sutcliffe, Maurice Leyland and Sir Len Hutton to Geoffrey Boycott, it has also had several of the ropiest on its books. George Deyes, a bowler who only batted as high as No. 10 if somebody was injured, had 17 innings for Yorkshire in 1907. Ten of these innings ended in scoreless ignominy, one more at 0 not out, two after just one run had been accumulated, and two more at 1 not out. He made one score of 4, but his last innings of the summer, against Sussex at Brighton on August 27, yielded 12 runs, before he was bowled by Vine. This double-figure glory was heady stuff for a natural No. 11 like Deyes, but it was hardly necessary. His effort was only the ninth highest score of the Yorkshire innings. His season's average of 1.42 would have been 0.61 without that last innings, which proved to be the final first-class innings of his career.

One member of Sir James Barrie's Allahakbarries Cricket Club was described as 'the worst batsman in the world, and equally at home with the ball', but even he never equalled the record of Peter Judge of Glamorgan. Playing against the Indian touring team on 11 June 1946, Judge was bowled by the leg-break bowler Chandra Sarwate first ball for 0. This brought the first Glamorgan innings to a close. As there was little time left, and the Indians, seeking a victory, enforced the follow-on, Glamorgan sportingly agreed to open the batting with the two men still out at the wicket, their veteran off-spinner John Clay, and Peter Judge. Judge faced the first ball of the second innings, also from Sarwate, and was cleaned bowled once again. Despite Judge's best efforts, Glamorgan managed to hold out for a draw.

Nobody has ever quite equalled this feat, though Surrey's Monte Lynch did achieve a pair before lunch against Middlesex in 1977. J. W. Harris of Nairobi was dismissed twice in two balls from C. J. Antrobus in 1939. Antrobus finished off Nairobi's first innings at the Gymkhana Ground with a hat-trick, including Harris as the third victim. As with Glamorgan against India, the follow-on was enforced and the men with pads on opened the second innings. Antrobus did not bowl the first over, during which four runs were scored, including a single by Harris. The demon spinner did, however, take the second over and, with his first ball, bowled the unfortunate Mr Harris for 1. C. J. had thus taken four wickets in four balls, including J. W. Harris twice. But at least Harris made one run in the process.

Errol Holmes, captain of Surrey, made 0 and 0 two years in succession for Surrey v. MCC, in 1947 and 1948. He lasted a total of six balls across the four innings. He retired at the end of the 1948 season, but had the satisfaction of knowing that, in the corresponding fixture in 1936, he had made 63 and 74.

Teams have been all out for 0 so often that it is no longer considered a curiosity. Even my home village of Saltwood once achieved this feat, against Martin Walters' XI on 25 May 1964. The heroes of the day, Bob Chappell (7 for 0) and Geoff Cooke (3 for 0), now play more golf than cricket, but their achievement is framed on the pavilion wall for all to see. The first recorded instance of

a scoreless innings was in August 1815, when Walsingham and Fakenham achieved this dire feat at the hands of Litcham, Dunham and Brisley: three villages ganging up against two. In Derbyshire in 1838, the village of Kegworth were dismissed for a mere 1, courtesy of the vicar's groom, and then got rid of their opponents, Diseworth, for 0. This is probably the lowest scoring full cricket match in history, although, in 1825, Five of Kent tied with Five of Sussex when each team was all out for 0. One T. Warner captured all the wickets for Sussex, after which T. Ayerst returned the favour for Kent.

Only ten runs were scored in the two-innings match between the Australian sides Mooroobark and Mullindillingong, in September 1888, and all of them came in Mullindillingong's first innings. It is recorded that a Mr Mummery made 8 of these runs. Mooroobark were then all out for 0, and in their second innings both teams failed to trouble the scorers (except that they had to try to spell the names of the two teams correctly). So Mullindillingong won by 10 runs.

In a twelve-a-side prep school match at Devonshire Park, Eastbourne, on 16 August 1883, Mr F. E. Howlett's side made 75, and then Mr A. B. Holman's team made 76. They went on to win by an innings and one run, for they dismissed Mr Howlett's side for 0 in their second innings, two boys being run out.

At the opposite end of the spectrum, the title of the World's Best Batsman has probably been secured for all time by Sir Donald Bradman (b. 1908). His achievements were head and shoulders above his contemporaries, and

no important batting record eluded him. However, even
his career, over two decades of run-gathering, pales into
obscurity when compared with that of Jack Hyams, the
World's Leading Runmaker. Between 1934 and 1990, he
scored over 112,000 runs at senior club level, for clubs
such as the Stoics, the Forty Club, London Counties and
Magdala. He hit 168 centuries, including at least one each
year for 55 years, his highest score being 199 not out in
an RAF match in 1944. In 1953 he scored 4,328 runs. Just
to make sure he was of value to his side, during his career
he also took 1,283 wickets.

Many times a batsman has scored all his side's runs,
beginning with that vicar's groom at Kegworth in 1838.
The most impressive effort seems to be that of Jonathan
Bramhill, in a schools Under-13 match for Gilling Castle
against Bramcote in 1980. He came in with Gilling Castle's
score at a precarious 0 runs for four wickets, and set
about the bowling to such an extent that he hit off all
the 43 runs required for victory, while at the other end
one more runless rabbit was returned to the hutch.
Nobody else who has scored all his side's runs appears
to have made more than 10 in the process, which was
what Sayes of St Christopher made against Letchworth
II in May 1939. J. Bond of Letchworth took all ten St
Christopher wickets for two runs.

Percy Chapman, who worked at Mackeson's Brewery
in Hythe while qualifying to play for Kent, scored 183
out of 201 for the Brewery against the Elham Division of
the Kent County Police on 8 September 1925, including
all of the first 150 runs scored. The next highest score

29

was 11, by Extras, and then 4 not out, by the No. 11, H. Rose. Chapman batted at No. 4, and was the only one of the first seven batsmen to score anything at all. It is said that the Kent police loved it. Richard Simons of West Herts scored the first 60 runs of his team's innings against Abbots Langley in 1978, and 'a lad named Wilkinson' scored 31 not out, in Esh Winning's total of 36 against North Bitchburn in a Durham County League (Junior Section) match in 1978. The other five runs were extras. Esh Winning ended up losing.

At the other end of the scale are the feats of such as Jock Sutherland, actually a New Zealander, although he sounds Scottish, who opened the innings for Wakatu against Nelson in the 1977–78 season. Wakatu were fairly soon all out for a mere 21, but opener Jock was undefeated, having watched the wickets tumble at the other end while he compiled a dour and parsimonious 0.

Big hitting is one of the most exciting features of batsmanship. Donald Bradman hit very few sixes in his career, yet he is credited with a century in minor cricket at Blackheath, New South Wales, in 1931–32 scored in only three eight-ball overs. It was a minor game against a team from Lithgow, and Bradman actually made 256, including 14 sixes and 29 fours. At one stage, in a three-over spell while batting with Oliver Wendell-Bill, he made 100 out of 102 added. In his own account, the strokes were:

(First over)	6,6,4,2,4,4,6,1	Total: 33
(Second over)	6,4,4,6,6,4,6,4	Total: 40
(Third over)	1,6,6,1,1,4,4,6	Total: 29

(The first and fifth balls of the third over were faced by Oliver Wendell-Bill.) The time taken for the hundred was estimated at less than 18 minutes, which until that time was considered the New South Wales record for hitting a hundred.

Bradman hit bizarre sixes from time to time, as well. *Smith's Weekly*, in 1921, reports that the youthful Bradman 'sent a ball over the boundary fence. It struck half a brick, rebounded onto a fence post, poised there for an appreciable time, and ran along the top of the palings the whole length of a panel of fencing before descending outside the boundary'. Even at the age of twelve or thirteen, Bradman knew how to hit a memorable boundary.

31

Six sixes in an over has been achieved twice in first-class cricket, firstly by Sir Garfield Sobers, off the unfortunate Malcolm Nash, for Nottinghamshire against Glamorgan in 1968, and then by R. J. Shastri, off one Tilak Raj, for Bombay against Baroda in 1985. In lower grades of cricket it is not uncommon, having been achieved for the first time on record by 'Honest Will' Caldecourt for Watford against The Rest of Hertfordshire in the 1850s. The first-class record for most sixes in an innings is held by the New Zealander John Reid, who hit 15 in his innings of 296 for Wellington against Northern Districts in 1962–63, and for most sixes in a season, almost inevitably, by Ian Botham, who hit 80 in 1985.

36 is not, however, the most runs scored in one over. The record is 77, off a 22-ball over bowled by Wellington and New Zealand batsman Robert Vance, during a Shell

Trophy match against Canterbury, at Christchurch on 20 February 1990. Vance's captain, Erwin McSweeney, instructed him to bowl a succession of no-balls to encourage the Canterbury batsmen to go for the runs required to win, in the hope that they would get out in the process. Vance bowled his over as a series of full-tosses from several yards up the pitch, to such a degree that the batsmen, Lee Germon and Roger Ford, were able to rattle up a Canterbury record ninth-wicket partnership of 182, before the match ended after all in a draw. The over went as follows: 144466461411666660040, out of which Germon hit 69 including eight sixes and five fours. Ewen Gray, bowling at the other end, had 17 taken off his final over of the game, and the scores ended level. Wellington had four points deducted as a result of their activities, and Vance's over was declared illegitimate. It does not, therefore, feature in the cricket record books, although Germon's score of 160 not out remains his highest to date.

Lesser but more legal totals have been compiled in one over. Three examples have cropped up in recent years. Kurt Jansen, a good Euro-cricketing name, playing for Northolt II against Ealing II on 10 May 1987, hit 41 off an over which contained two no-balls. He hit six sixes, a four and a single to keep the strike for the next over. Simon Walker of Honley, in Division II of the Huddersfield League, hit 40 in one over from James Moulson of Meltham on 13 June 1992. He hit six sixes and one four in the over, which included just one no-ball. Two weeks later, Nigel Bruce of Marlow Park hit 38 (5 sixes, 2 fours) off an over from John Greenacombe which included one no-ball. Mike Thornton, playing for the Highway Club against Alvis of Coventry in 1986, took 38 off an over from Peter Stanyer. He hit five consecutive sixes, but the sixth ball was a no-ball, and he could only score two off it. He hit the seventh, legitimate, delivery for six, but was out off the next ball he received.

The South African Test cricketer Dudley Nourse, playing for a South African XI against the Military Police at Cairo in 1942, hit nine sixes off consecutive balls, and 11 in 12 balls, an unparalleled feat of fast scoring. Basil D'Oliveira, playing for Croxley against Mariedahl in Cape Town in 1953–54, scored 225 in 65 minutes, including 28 sixes and 10 fours, meaning that he only had to run 17 of his runs. The rest of his team scored 11 runs between them. In another game in South Africa, the young D'Oliveira hit 81 for St Augustine against Trafalgar CC, including 46 off one eight-ball over, with seven sixes and one four. Richard Banks, playing in a seven-a-side competition for the Six Bells pub in Boreham, Essex against the Prince of Wales, Inworth, in May 1987, hit 193 off 40 balls in the first round of a brewery competition. He hit 24 sixes, 12 fours, and just one single. He left three balls completely untouched while he got his breath back. Even in a seven-a-side competition, that is worth a pint or two.

Tony Naseer, playing for Bradford Gymkhana CC on 12 July 1986, scored 107 in 23 minutes. He hit eight fours and 12 sixes, as well as three singles. He explained that he was in a hurry to meet his sister at Manchester airport later that afternoon. However, he was still thirty minutes late for her flight.

The record for the most runs off one ball is a highly disputed title. In Bonbury, Western Australia, a hit for 286 was recorded at the end of the last century. The ball got lodged in a tree. The record in England seems to be 34, scored at Brighton Racecourse in 1892, but the achievement of Brian Lefson at Portsmouth in 1962 is surely unique. Lefson, a South African, had recently arrived in Britain and had played several games for Romany CC as an off-spinner, without ever getting a bat. Finally, against United Services, his chance came. He was so thrilled about his first innings in England that he forgot the elementary rules of running between the wickets. His first ball he hit stylishly and off the meat of the bat, straight to mid-on. There would be no run there under normal circumstances, but these were not normal circumstances. Lefson, in his excitement, called for a run. Mid-on, startled by this lunatic call, took a shy at the bowler's wicket, and missed. Two overthrows resulted, but the second of these runs looked very risky to extra cover, who had fielded mid-on's wild throw, so he hurled the ball hard at the wicketkeeper. This throw, too, was off target, and poor short leg, trying to back up the wicketkeeper, could only slow the ball down. He turned and chased it, while the batsmen ran on. Short leg, compounding his original error of half a stop, now made half a throw, to the bowler, who was to be seen holding his head in his hands as his analysis crumbled before his eyes. The throw was, of course, inaccurate, and it ran all the way to the boundary for four more overthrows. During all this excitement, there had been one short run as the batsmen negotiated the balls and fielders bounding in all directions, so in the end, the umpires decided that only seven runs had been scored. Two curiosities had been achieved. Firstly, the bowler had been hit for seven the ball after taking a wicket; secondly, the batsman had scored seven off his first ball ever received outside Africa.

Fred Geeson of Leicestershire holds the record for the highest score ever made three innings in a row. His final three innings of the 1899 season were 32 against Derbyshire, and then 32 and 32 against Warwickshire. Nobody has ever made a higher score three times running than Geeson's 32. Tom Hayward, the great Surrey opening bat, made three scores of 144 in 1906, but not in consecutive innings. Javad Miandad hit 200 not out twice for Glamorgan in 1981, but not in consecutive innings. This appears to be the highest score to have been made twice in a season by the same batsman. The highest score to have been made twice in a career by one man is 302, by Walter Hammond, who took the runs off the Glamorgan bowlers on both occasions. In 1934, he was undefeated at that score, but on 1 June 1939, he was out, c. Haydn Davies, b. Emrys Davies. Emrys Davies went on to make 287 not out in Glamorgan's reply, so the match was drawn (which is not much of a curiosity).

T. L. Brierley, playing for Glamorgan against Lancashire at Old Trafford on 14 June 1938, scored 116, the highest score of his career. Glamorgan still lost, by nine wickets. After the war, he switched counties and, playing for Lancashire against Glamorgan at Liverpool on 12 June 1947, made 116 not out, which thus became the joint highest score of his entire career. Brierley's only century for Lancashire did his new county little good. The match was drawn.

Lastly, the ultimate in hard luck stories. A club cricketer, signing himself 'Mauvaise Chance', wrote to *The Cricketer* in August 1927 as follows: 'Towards the end of last season, I, who am a bowler, had made 96 runs towards my first century. In turning to hit the ball to the leg boundary (where it duly arrived, wide of any fielder, to score the necessary four runs) the top strap of my left pad, which had become unfastened without my noticing it, flicked off my leg bail, and it was held that as this occurred in the making of a stroke, I was out – trodden on my wicket. I am not sure whether the decision was just, but in any case out I went, score 96. I shall never get near it again. An occasional fifty when the gods are kind, but that is all.' The most poignant aspect of the letter is that it took him almost a full year to bear to put pen to paper.

OVERTHROWS

0 out of eighth-wicket partnership of 93
S. Abrahams (Alma Marist) v. Western Province, 1987

6 off the last ball to win a county match
R. E. S. Wyatt (aged 50) off H. T. F. Buse, Worcestershire v.
Somerset at Taunton, 24 Aug 1951

9 runs scored off last ball of match for victory
David Cox (Chipping Sodbury) v. Patchway CC, 28 Jun 1988

10 runs off one ball in first-class cricket
A. N. Hornby off J. Street, Lancashire v. Surrey, The Oval, 14
Jul 1873
S. Wood off C. J. Burnup, Derbyshire v. MCC, Lord's, 26 May
1900

42 in an innings, all in boundaries
A. Watt, Kent v. Nottinghamshire, Trent Bridge, 1933

44 in an innings, all in boundaries
P. Marner, Lancashire v. Nottinghamshire, Southport, 23 Aug
1960

48 in an innings, all in boundaries
J.E. Emburey, England XI v Tasmania, Hobart, 20 Dec 1986

50 off 9 balls
D. L. Hays, Quidnuncs v. Royal Navy, Portsmouth, 1978

50 off 10 balls
Stephen Downes (aged 14), Styal U-15 v. Holmes Chapel
U-15, 1977

100 out of 112
D. Walpole, Hockley v. Brentwood Radio Station, 1965

104 out of 110
H. E. Dollery (aged 16), Reading School v. MCC, 1931

112 runs in an innings without a single boundary
R. Iddison, Yorkshire v. Cambridgeshire, Hunslet, Jul 1869

141* out of 169
G. M. Turner, Worcestershire v. Glamorgan, Swansea, 30 Jun
1977

200 out of 298
T. W. Graveney, Gloucestershire v. Glamorgan, Newport, 8 Aug 1956

202 out of 261
Cecil Holden, Birkenhead Park v. Northern, 11 Jul 1896

203 not out before lunch
H. J. J. Malcolm, Stoics v. HMS *Dolphin*, The Oval, 1948

204 in boundaries in innings of 205
(18 sixes, 24 fours and 1 single) Paul Morgan (Balgownie 4th XI) v. University, 1991

206* out of 228
Duncan Falconer, Ewell v. Dorking, 31 Jul 1988

207 on only first-class appearance
N. Calloway, New South Wales v. Queensland, 1913–14

214* as batsman's only Test score over 50
D. Lloyd (Lancs), England v. India, Edgbaston, 1974

286 out of 321
A. C. Richards, 'E' Company v. 'A' Company, 2nd Hampshire Regiment, 1901

298 by a woman
Jan Molyneaux, Olympic v. Northcote, Melbourne, 1967

309* out of 362
Tony Tillbrook, St Thomas v. Trinibis, Waltham Abbey

645 runs without being out
G. A. Hick: successive scores of 171*, 69*, 252*, 100*, 53 for Worcestershire, Jul 1990

709 runs without being out
K. C. Ibrahim: successive scores of 218*, 36*, 234*, 78*, 144, 1947–48

1,006 runs in 3 innings
Chaman Lal Malhotra: successive scores of 502*, 360, 144, Mehandra College, Patiala, Nov 1956

1,013 runs in 4 innings
W. H. Ponsford: successive scores of 437, 202, 38, 336 for Victoria, 1927–28

BATTING TO REMEMBER

1,294 runs in a month, including three consecutive ducks
L. Hutton, Jun 1949

All run 6 at Lord's
T. G. Evans, Players v. Gentlemen, 1949

All run 6 in a Test Match
M. A. Atherton, England v. Pakistan, 1992

Ball hit down school chimney into classroom
Wallasey Grammar School, 23 Jun 1955

Bowled for 199 just after partner had run one run short
W. Rhodes, Yorkshire v. Sussex, Hove, Aug 1909

Final 84 runs of innings of 143, all boundaries
H. Gimblett, Somerset v. Northamptonshire, Bath, 1936

Maiden Test century reached with a six
Paul Winslow (South Africa) v. England, Old Trafford, 9 Jul 1955

No ducks by one team in an entire Test series
New Zealand v. England, 1949 (4 Tests)

Top of first-class batting averages seven seasons in a row
W. R. Hammond (Glos), 1933 to 1939 inclusive

Two left-handers scoring double hundreds in same innings
E. Davies (215) and W. E. Jones (212), Glamorgan v. Essex, Brentwood, 16 Jun 1948

Two hundreds in a day
R. G. Ormsby, Schenectady CC of New York, Montreal, 25 Jul 1930
Tim McVey, 101* for Penrith QE GS (a.m.), and 108 for Penrith 3rd XI v. Gamblesby (p.m.), 1977
J. H. Curtis, for Monmouth v. MCC (a.m.), and for Usk (p.m.), 1906
C. C. Dacre, 111 for N. Shore School, Auckland (a.m.), and 120 for N. Shore 4th XI (p.m.)
K. S. Ranjitsinhji, Sussex v. Yorkshire, Brighton, 1896

Three hundreds in a day
K. S. Ranjitsinhji, 128 for Cassandra v. Saffron Walden, 132 for the Basinettes, and 150 for Long Vacation XI, all at Cambridge, probably 1890

BIO-DIVERSITY:
ANIMALS IN
CRICKET

Since the earliest days of cricket, this best-loved game has been a source of constant danger to the animal kingdom. At Lord's in the early years of the Marylebone ground, a ball from George Brown of Brighton killed a dog 'after passing through longstop's coat'. It is not absolutely clear from the syntax of the report whether it was the ball or the dog which passed through longstop's coat, but if the former was the case, it is remarkable that, in the days of underarm bowling, it was possible to deliver the ball with sufficient ferocity to kill a dog and rip longstop's outer garments to shreds. However, he was obviously quick. One of Brown's longstops, called Dench, used to field with a sack of straw tied to his chest.

In May 1821, it was reported that 'a carter of Mrs Rose of Stanlake was fined £4 and dismissed her service for having left the care of his horse to go to cricket, by which neglect a valuable cart-horse was gored to death by a vicious cow'. No animal bigger than a horse has yet been confirmed as having been killed as a direct result of a game of cricket, but it seems probable that harm has come to several elephants over the course of the history of the game in the Indian subcontinent and in Africa.

The only animal to be featured in the Obituary columns of *Wisden* is Peter the Cat. In its 1965 edition, the cricketers' bible records the death of 'CAT, PETER, whose ninth life ended on November 5, 1964'. It goes on to say that Peter was 'well-known to cricket-watchers at Lord's, where he spent 12 of his 14 years. He preferred a close-up view of the proceedings, and his sleek black form could often be seen prowling on the field of play when the crowds were biggest.' In a moving tribute, the then Secretary of MCC, Mr S. C. Griffith, said, 'he was a cat of great character and loved publicity'.

Birds are the most common of cricket's corpses. The well-documented and well-stuffed sparrow in the museum at Lord's was killed on 3 July 1936 by a ball bowled by Jehangir Khan of Cambridge University to T. N. Pearce, playing for MCC, but that is by no means the only bird killed and stuffed in the furtherance of cricket. During the Nottinghamshire v Middlesex match of 1866, Tom Hearne of Middlesex was about to bowl when he saw a pigeon overhead, and decided to throw the ball at it. He brought it down 'dead as a doornail'. The bird was stuffed and preserved as a family heirloom. When Major H. C. Dent was batting for Charlton Park CC against Felsted Long Vacation CC in 1888, 'a fast ball was put down to me', as he recorded in a letter he wrote to *The Times* in 1919, 'which I seemed to lose sight of, but was fortunate enough to put through the slips for two. A dead swallow with a broken beak was then found midway down the pitch; the bird had evidently flown headlong into the ball.' This bird, too, was sent to the taxidermist, and 'subsequently was on view in the Charlton Park clubhouse for many years'. The bowler in question was one A. H. Pease, and this seems to be the only time that runs have been scored off a ball that killed a bird.

Two batsmen have been recorded as bowled by balls that hit a bird on their way from the bowler's hand. Another Major, this time called Bentinck, was playing at Alton in Hampshire when a ball from Roberts killed a swallow and went on to dislodge the bails. *The Cricketer* also reports that at Roydon in Essex, in 1910, E. G. Rust was bowling to his son when there was 'a precisely similar occurrence except that the bird was a sedge warbler'. In both cases the batsman was too surprised to get his bat in the way of the ball. On 22 November 1969, John Inverarity of Western Australia was bowled by a ball which hit a swallow in mid-flight and was deflected on to his stumps. The bowler was Greg Chappell of South Australia, but the umpire signalled a no-ball. More appropriately, it should have been given as a dead ball, as Chappell's delivery was entirely fair. Inverarity had at the time not yet scored, but after the death of the swallow gave him another life, he went on to make 89. As *Wisden* reported, it was truly a case of 'Duck Saved by Swallow'.

Other cricketers responsible for the death of birds include G. A. Smithson of Leicestershire, whose drive killed a bird hopping along the boundary at Worcester in 1953, and D. Ramsamooj of Northamptonshire, who slaughtered a pigeon during an innings of 44 at The Oval in July 1963 in a similar fashion. C. J. Knott of Hampshire killed a butterfly with a ball bowled against Gloucestershire at Portsmouth in August 1951.

There is a trophy which signifies the avian world's ultimate sacrifice to cricket, for it is made of an emu's egg. What happened to the emu which ought to have come out of the egg is not recorded, but the trophy is now at Lord's in the MCC museum. It was presented by Messrs Spiers and Pond (sponsors of the 1861–62 tour by H. H. Stephenson's team to Australia, and thus commercial ancestors of Benson & Hedges, Schweppes and NatWest) to William Burrup, then Secretary of Surrey CCC, with the simple inscription, 'S&P to W.B., Melbourne 1882'.

Sparrows, swallows, rooks and swifts as well as pigeons and emus have met their fate at cricket matches, but there is at least one heart-warming instance of a sparrow which cheated death by moments. When MCC played the Australians at Lord's in 1902, the Australian fast bowler Ernest Jones, fielding at mid-off, flicked the ball at a sparrow and stunned it. Albert Craig, a Yorkshireman renowned as 'The Surrey Poet' for the doggerel verses he used to sell at The Oval, went to administer the *coup de*

grâce to the injured bird but, just as he reached it, the bird recovered its senses and flew off, much to the delight of the crowd.

Fish are not safe from the well-struck cricket ball either. Mr Thornton Berry records a half-pound grayling killed by a six-hit (at least the fish was in season); and at a match in Sohar, recalled by the umpire Mr R. Townshend Stephens in *The Times* of 12 July 1934, 'a ball was hit for six into the sea; but it fell not into the sea, for it was swallowed by a shark. I gave the man out. "c. Fish b. Birkat Ullah" was duly entered in the scorebook by a soldier clerk.'

A less fortunate shark was the one encountered by PC Kevin Sansom in New Zealand late in 1985. The seven-foot shark had moved in close to swimmers at a beach at Invercargill on the southern tip of the South Island, so PC Sansom attacked it with a cricket bat. The stunned shark was dragged ashore, where it died. In 1986, at Bristol, a dead mackerel stopped play. During the Old Cliftonians v. Stowe Templars match in the first round of the Cricketer Cup, Simon Hazlitt's innings for the Old Cliftonians was interrupted by a dead mackerel falling from the sky and narrowly missing his head. It had been dropped by a seagull, which had stolen it from a sealion tank at Bristol Zoo. Hazlitt was not too disturbed, though, and went on to make the top score for his side, 45, as Old Cliftonians beat Stowe Templars by three wickets.

Fishes are not the only beasts to have taken part in a cricket match. In Nairobi, there was a well-documented case of 'lion stopped play'. The ball was hit towards the boundary, which in those days was surrounded by bush. As the fielder chased the ball, a lion suddenly appeared on the pitch and began playing with the ball. As it had neither gone over the boundary line nor disappeared from sight, the umpires were reluctant to signal either 'lost ball' or four runs. The batsmen clocked up an unrecorded number of runs before the fielding side summoned up courage enough to chase off the lion and retrieve the somewhat chewed ball.

The match between Launceston and Old Suttonians, at Launceston, Cornwall, in August 1984, was stopped by camels strolling on to the field of play from a nearby circus no fewer than four times during the afternoon. A pair of black bulls charged across the pitch during the first match of the 1987 season at Swardeston, Norfolk. Batsmen and fielders fled. An iguana stopped play during the first match between Young Sri Lanka and Young England on 5 February 1987, when it 'crept menacingly across the middle of the historic Columbo Cricket Club ground'. A snake held up proceedings by slithering across the wicket during a school practice game at Cowell, South Australia, in 1967–68. The batsman, one Tony Wiseman, let the ball pass but stepped out of his ground to kill the metre-long snake with his bat. There was no appeal for a stumping, as the wicketkeeper had fled.

The Hon. Lionel Tennyson is probably the only England cricket captain to have shot dead a goat while on official duty. While touring India in 1937–38, the Jam Sahib of Jamnagar invited the England captain to accompany him on a leopard hunt. A goat was tied to a stake in a clearing, and all sat silently waiting till the leopard appeared. When at last a leopard stalked cautiously towards the ill-fated goat, the Jam Sahib pressed a musket into the hands of the guest of honour, who aimed carefully at the leopard, and shot the goat. It was an act of kindness to both the goat, who would otherwise have died a horrible death, and the leopard, who escaped to fight another day. As Ian Peebles records, 'this slight setback gave all concerned, including the marksman, infinitely more pleasure than the usual result of a live goat and a dead leopard, and next day Lionel received a cable from White's Club offering to pay its passage home if he would have the goat stuffed'.

On 21 May 1827, a match took place on Harefield Common near Rickmansworth, Hertfordshire, between Two Gentlemen of Middlesex and Mr Francis Trumper, a farmer at Harefield, with the help of his sheep-dog. *The Times* records that 'in the first innings the two gentlemen got three runs, and Mr Trumper three for himself and two for his dog. In the second innings, the two gentlemen again got three runs, and Mr Trumper then going in, and getting two runs, beat the two gentlemen leaving two wickets standing'. Before the match, the odds were 5 to 1 against Farmer Trumper, but after the first innings the odds were shortened to 4 to 1 on the man-dog combination. The dog, who remains unnamed, proved to be a very quick fielder. He stood obediently near his master as the ball was delivered, and 'the moment the ball was hit he kept his eye upon it, and started off after it with speed'. On fielding the ball, the dog would run back to his master and give the ball back to his master 'with such wonderful quickness, that the gentlemen found it difficult to get a run even from a very long hit'.

Earlier in the century, it was said, not entirely in fun, that John Willes, his sister Christina and their dog 'could beat any eleven in England'. Willes, with the help of his sister, was the originator of round-arm bowling.

In a Gloucestershire garden, in the 1850s, three dogs achieved cricketing immortality by fielding with enthusiasm and skill as five brothers learned their cricket. The brothers were Henry, Alfred, Edward, William Gilbert and Fred Grace, and the dogs were called Don, Ponto and Noble. As Bernard Darwin wrote in his appreciation of W. G. Grace, 'they were particularly useful when the ball was hit into the woods or the water.' Things had changed from Hambledon days. In 1773, posters advertising a great match clearly stated that 'dogs will be shot'.

Dogs occasionally get their own back. Nottinghamshire and England wicketkeeper Bruce French was bitten by a dog while out jogging during England's tour of the West Indies in 1985–86. And there was at least one dog which behaved itself as a spectator. R. A. H. Mitchell's dog at Eton College died in 1889, and the *Eton College Chronicle* for 30 November of that year includes a poem entitled 'In Memoriam Boni Canis', which, for those without a classical education, is translated as 'In Memory of a Good Dog', or, more subtly, 'In Memory of Boney the Dog', for that was the late hound's name.

48

> They say, who watched him at a match,
> He shuddered at a careless stroke;
> Appraised the balls that shot, that broke
> And barked approval at a catch.

On 7 July 1962, on what proved to be the final day's play in the Third Test at Headingley between England and Pakistan, play was halted during the morning session by a boxer dog called Brutus. He invaded the pitch at the end of an over, evaded all attempts of the players to catch him, seemed to be surrounded by three constables before jinking to one side and causing one of the policemen to crash to the ground amid much applause, and then ran off through the gate at the Kirkstall Lane end. This was the second consecutive year in which Brutus, who lived opposite the ground, had interrupted the Test match, and both times England went on to win.

The following year, the example of Brutus had spread as far afield as the south coast. At Hove on 18 June 1963, Ian Thomson of Sussex was awarded four when a shot off Alf Valentine of the West Indies was fielded by a dog.

He went on to make 35. The same thing happened at
Southampton on 22 August (though probably involving a
different dog) when Keith Andrew, the Northamptonshire wicketkeeper, was awarded four runs during
his innings of 32 against Hampshire when the ball was
once again fielded by a dog. The match between Southern
Schools and The Rest at Lord's on 5 August 1963 was
stopped briefly when a black cat, called Sinbad, strolled
on to the wicket. He proved unlucky for The Rest, who
were batting at the time. B. H. White performed the hat-
trick for the Southern Schools, who went on to win by
10 wickets.

OVERTHROWS

Ball eaten by cow
Kentisbeare v. Exmouth, Kentisbeare, 1989

Dog stopped play
Yorkshire v. Surrey, Bradford, Jun 1979

Fielder jumped on bystander's horse and rode after ball
Tunbridge Wells, 1833

Fifteen weasels crossed wicket during match
Darlington, 1895

Flock of sheep on pitch stopped play
Glamorgan v. Gloucestershire, Ebbw Vale, 4 Aug 1948

Flying ants stopped play
Chard v. Sampford Arundel, Chard, 11 Aug 1990

Grasshoppers stopped play
South Australia v. Queensland, Adelaide, Dec 1947

Grayling killed by ball
S. Raine, Hawes v. Aysgarth, River Yore, Jul 1934

Jacko the Monkey stopped play
MCC v. Maharashtra, Poona, 21 Dec 1951

Pitch sabotaged by horses
at Tintwistle (Cheshire), 1976

Runaway horse and cart stopped play
MCC v. Yorkshire, Scarborough, 30 Aug 1892

Stoat crossed wicket during match
Cambridge Victoria v. Royston, Royston, 1890

Stoats stopped play
Mumbles v. Skewen, Mumbles, Aug 1989

Swarm of bees stopped play
Bickley Park v. Band of Brothers, Bickley Park, 1887
Oxford U. v. Worcestershire, The Parks, Jun 1962
Lampeter v. Bronwydd, Lampeter, Jun 1988

BOWLING TO
REMEMBER

The first prerequisite of a successful bowler is self-confidence. Clarrie Grimmett, the New Zealander who became perhaps Australia's greatest spin bowler, wrote in his 1930 book, *Getting Wickets,* that 'I bowled remarkably well, and was even congratulated by my opponents.' That was after a hard day's work for South Australia against New South Wales in December 1925, when he took 0 for 174. Perhaps his opponents were a sarcastic bunch, congratulating anybody who gave them the chance to score a lot of runs on flat wickets, but Grimmett's certainty that he was a great bowler was justified. He took 200 wickets in fewer Tests than anybody who has reached that target, despite not making his first Test appearance until he was 34 years old.

Other great bowlers, like Fred Trueman and Sydney Barnes, have not been shy about their own skills, either. Trueman has described himself as 'the finest fast bowler that ever drew breath'. When S. F. Barnes once spent a rare day in the field without taking many wickets, he was heard to remark, 'They aren't batting well enough to get out.' Batsmen facing Harold Larwood gave themselves out from time to time, after playing and missing, 'You didn't touch it,' said the wicketkeeper. 'Maybe not, but I'm going all the same,' replied the terrified batsman.

Gloucestershire's Alan Walker was disappointed, not to say gutted, not to win the Man of the March award in his county's Sunday League game against Northants on 9 June 1991. The match, at Moreton-in-Marsh, was abandoned in a torrential downpour after just one ball, bowled by Walker. After the match, Walker was positive about his contribution to the match. 'I reckon I deserve the award. It was a damn fine delivery, moved a bit in the air, seamed off the pitch and all he could do was play it back to me. In fact, I was the only man to touch the ball in the entire match.'

The ultimate in bowling success is to take all ten wickets in an innings, a feat which has been done many times. Some have done it with more of a flourish than others, of course. John MacIldowie, playing for Southgate against Barnet on 18 June 1932, took all ten wickets clean bowled for only 22 runs, after first dropping a catch off another bowler. He must have had to buy a

few rounds of drinks in the bar that night.

The feat of bowling all ten batsmen, as John Mac-Ildowie did, has been accomplished many times in minor cricket, at least fifty times up to the First War, according to a report in *The Cricketer* for November 1978, by somebody who apparently needs sixty years to compile his figures. It has only happened once in first-class cricket, done by John Wisden, the originator of the Almanack, playing for the North against the South at Lord's in 1850. Another curiosity about this feat is that Wisden was born in Brighton but was playing for the North. The probable explanation is that he had recently acquired an interest in a ground at Leamington Spa, which is well north of Watford, and thus he was deemed to be a wild Northerner. Eric Hollies, the Warwickshire leg-spinner, is the only other first-class cricketer to have taken all ten without the assistance of another player. Against Nottinghamshire at Birmingham in 1946 he took all ten for 49 runs, bowling seven Nottinghamshire players, and trapping the other three leg before wicket.

Several cricketers have dismissed all eleven players in a 12-a-side match (the names of P. H. Morton, T. W. Dyson, G. Wallace and F. Shacklock immediately spring to mind), but the most spectacular domination of the bowling figures was that of Chris Tinley, a lob bowler who played for Nottinghamshire and All England. He delivered his underarm balls 'hip high and at a fair pace' and his success against any but the best opposition was phenomenal. Against Eighteen of Hallam in July 1860, Tinley took all 17 wickets.

The quickest 'all ten' was undoubtedly achieved by H. Highley, later to become a man of the cloth, at school in the 1870s. In his rapid achievement he was undoubtedly helped by the school umpires' rather feeble grasp of the Laws. According to a letter he wrote to *The Cricketer* in 1939, he opened the bowling for the fourth House XI in a junior competition. In his first over, he took two wickets, which so pleased his captain that he asked him to take the second over as well. So Highley switched ends and took four more wickets in this over. His captain, even more pleased with the way things were going, suggested Master Highley take the third over as well, during which he took the remaining four wickets. He thus became the only bowler ever to take all ten when no other player bowled at all. His reason for writing to *The Cricketer* was not to show off his prowess, for, as he wrote, 'the opposing batsmen under no circumstances would have played if cricket had not been compulsory', but to ask whether it was legal for one player to bowl three consecutive overs. *The Cricketer* replied that it was not, although in the 1870s it would have been possible to bowl two overs in a row.

Old fogeys writing to cricket magazines are the source of some of the curiouser curiosities. 'Septuagenarian' wrote to *The Cricketer* on 10 May 1958 and reported that in a school match between Pocklington and Leeds Grammar School in 1900, one Miles d'Anson took all ten wickets bowling lobs. He wondered whether this was the only instance of all ten being taken by a lob bowler since overarm bowling was legalized in 1864. He reported that d'Anson, who died in the Great War, had injured his arm, which is why he bowled underarm.

But d'Anson is not unique. Charles Absolon, playing for Wood Green v. United Willesden on 21 July 1872, at the age of 55, took 18 of the 20 wickets as a bowler (10 bowled, 6 caught and 2 hit wicket), and for good measure caught the other two batsmen off somebody else's bowling. He weighed 15 stone at the time, and bowled lobs. He also took all ten wickets in 1873, for St Mary's Cray against Shoreham on 11 June that year, setting a standard that d'Anson (and quite possibly others, although nobody told *The Cricketer* in 1958 of other cases) could only equal.

The most unfortunate failure to get all ten was surely that of F. Green, playing for Radlett II against St Albans II at Clarence Park, St Albans, in 1939. He took nine wickets for one run, and the tenth batsman retired hurt, having been hit in the face by a ball from Green, which rose unexpectedly from a length. A similar achievement was recorded by Antiguan Vaughan Walsh, playing for Leicester Nomads in 1991. He took nine wickets for four runs, including five wickets with successive balls, but was denied all ten because the opposition's last man refused to bat against him. The acoustically named Martin Stereo took all ten wickets for one run for Hambledon against Petersfield on 16 June 1985. The last wicket almost fell to another bowler, but a shout put the would-be catcher off. How apt that a noise from one side or the other should ensure a Stereo ten-wicket haul.

One better than all ten wickets is, of course, all 20 in

a two-innings match. F. R. Spofforth, 'The Demon', did it in Australia in 1881, as did one J. Bryant, playing for Erskine v. the Deaf Mutes at Melbourne at around the same time. Jim Pothecary, of Western Province and South Africa, took all 20 in a club match in Cape Town in 1950–51, and Richie Benaud's father, Louis, a first-grade cricketer with the Cumberland club in New South Wales, took all 20 with his leg-breaks in the 1930s.

56

Paul Hugo, at school in South Africa in February 1931, and S. Fleming, at Marlborough College in 1967, are probably not the only people to have taken nine wickets in nine balls, and at least four bowlers have managed eight wickets in eight balls, two of them playing military matches in wartime. S. Vunisakiki, playing for Lomaloma against HMS *Leith* at Suva, Fiji, in the winter of 1939–40 was one. The other, Private J. Leake of the 9th Brigade, Canadian Expeditionary Force, playing against the Canadian ASC in France in 1917, went on from his eight in eight balls to take all ten in twelve balls. We must assume his side won.

Six wickets in an over was achieved by J. C. Yeoward in a Shrewsbury School Under-16 match in 1948. All his victims were bowled. Ben Sangster, aged 12, playing for Holmwood Prep School, near Liverpool, against a school from Lytham, also bowled six people in an over, in 1975. Noel Jones once took five wickets in consecutive balls, a feat that several cricketers have done over the years. However, Mr Jones's feat is unique in that he did it on his birthday, Christmas Day 1947, playing for the Yule Logs against Noel Bennett's XI at Preston Park, Brighton.

As the wickets tumbled in the freezing conditions, he must have thought that all his Christmasses and all his birthdays had come at once.

Hat-tricks are so uncurious these days that there is no point in recording them. One exception must be E. F. Mellor, who in 1947 (a fine year for multiple wicket-takers, it seems) took three wickets in consecutive balls while playing for his home village of Perry Street against Axminster. The following year, for Perry Street against Forton, he did the same thing. The only difference was that in 1947 he was bowling left-handed, and in 1948 he was bowling right-handed. Apparently Mr Perry was equally adept with either hand, and often switched in the middle of an over. There were two other players who bowled happily with either hand. Jack Harry, who played for Australia against England at Adelaide in January 1895, was able to bowl with either hand (although he did not bowl in his one Test: fellow debutant A. E. Trott took eight England wickets in the second innings to win the game by the massive margin of 382 runs; Trott was picked but did not bowl at all in the next Test). The other was William Yardley, one of the greatest batsmen of the 1870s, who bowled alternately with his left and right hand while playing for the Butterflies against Harrow School on 22 June 1872. It is not recorded whether this original style of bowling met with any success.

Alan Smith was Warwickshire's wicketkeeper for many years, before going on to become a power in cricket's ruling hierarchy, but in 1965 he wrote himself into the oddball section of cricket's records by abandoning his wicketkeeping gloves on 6 August in the match against Essex at Clacton, and achieving the hat-trick. They were no rabbits, either. He dismissed both openers, Barker and Smith, and the No. 4 batsmen, one Keith Fletcher. He took a fourth wicket, that of Trevor Bailey, in the course of 21 overs, but Essex held on for a draw.

It is at this point that I record my own personal Curiosity. While playing for Heartaches CC against the Waggoners CC at Abingdon on 22 June 1975, two stunningly inept Waggoners batsmen fell to my directionally challenged left-arm over the wicket medium-pace trundle, off the final two balls of the over. These were the seventh and eighth wickets to fall. The next over was bowled by local airline pilot, farmer and chiropracter Chris Cliff, and the even more inept remaining Waggoners batsmen chose the first two balls of the over to lob simple catches to where I stood at mid-on, both of which, amazing to relate, were safely held. Thus the final four wickets in the innings had fallen in four balls, and two bowlers were left on a hat-trick, one of whom had been involved, as bowler or fielder, in all four dismissals. The event becomes less of a curiosity when it is revealed that, despite this extraordinary feat, we went on to lose the match by 22 runs. It is also possibly less of a curiosity than the efforts of A. Townsend and K. Phillips, playing for Tamworth-in-Arden against Knowle and Dorridge in 1980. Townsend took three wickets, all clean bowled, with the last three balls of his over, and then Phillips took three wickets, also clean bowled, with the first and

only three of the next over, to dismiss Knowle and Dorridge for 15. Boringly, Tamworth went on to win.

When Chris Lewis began the Fourth Test at Headingley against Pakistan in 1992 with two wides off his first two balls, many assumed that this was some kind of record. They had forgotten the Third Test against Australia at Old Trafford in 1934, when G. O. B. Allen bowled the first over for England. It lasted for thirteen balls, including four no-balls and three wides. Gladstone Small, playing for Warwickshire against Middlesex at Coventry in 1982, bowled an 18-ball over, which included 11 no-balls and a wide. This remains the non-deliberate first-class record.

Curtly Ambrose, playing for Northamptonshire against Hampshire, bowled a 13-ball over in the last but one first-class match to be played at Dean Park, Bournemouth, on 17 August 1992. His over included seven no-balls, two of which dismissed batsman Kevin Shine, once 'caught' and once 'bowled'. He also conceded 12 runs, and Shine ended the day undefeated. This over came shortly after

Hampshire had lost six wickets for one run, slumping from 79 for 3 to 80 for 9, but Ambrose helped Hampshire to three-figure respectability. Despite Ambrose's generosity, Hampshire still went down to Northamptonshire by ten wickets.

W. H. Cawston, opening the bowling for Kettering Town against G. S. Robertson's (Notts) XI in August 1927, bowled just one over, but it lasted for 17 balls. It included 10 wides and one no-ball, but as none of the six legitimate deliveries were scored off, he ended up with an analysis of 1-1-0-0.

Perhaps an even less popular bowler with his captain was V. Norbury of Lancashire, who was bowling to Miles Howell of Surrey at the finish of their county match at Old Trafford on 18 July 1922. With Surrey needing just two runs to win, Norbury bowled to Howell, who was caught. But the umpire had shouted no-ball, so Howell was not out, and the scores were level. Norbury bowled the next ball to Howell, who was caught once again. And once again the umpire called no-ball, so Surrey had won and Howell remained not out.

OVERTHROWS

0 for 52 by bowler, all runs scored by one batsman
H. M. Barnard (Hants) off R. H. D. Sellers (Australians), Southampton, 14 Jul 1964

4 wickets in 4 balls by a Dane playing for an English team in Luxembourg
Ib Hucklecamp v. Optimists, 19 Jul 1976

5 wickets in an over without a hat-trick (w,w,-,w,nb,w,w)
Ross Chiese, Stanmore v. Radlett, 1980

5 wickets in 5 balls, and a catch dropped off the sixth
Graham Bouwer, Vereeniging v. Meyerton, SA, Dec 89

5 wickets in 5 balls to win match
Roddy Cowles, Ockley v. Barnes Green, 1979
(Barnes Green needed 4 off last 5 balls with 5 wkts in hand)

7 wickets in 7 balls to win match
E. C. Hoddinott, Evercreech v. King's Bruton, 10 Jun 1979

9 wickets in 12 balls, including 7 in 7 balls
Shaun Wilson, Elsenham v. White Horse, Harlow, 1987

10 for 58, then 10 for 15 in consecutive matches
Lionel Jones (aged 47) Shere v. Hove Montefiore, 1 Sep 1985
                          Shere v. Motspur Park, 7 Sep 1985

10 wickets for 1 run in 14 balls, including 7 in 7 balls
Ken Maxwell, Marchington v. Trentside, 5 May 1985

11 for 96 in only Test match
C. S. Marriott, England v. West Indies, The Oval, 1933

105 consecutive dot balls
H. L. Hazell, Somerset v Gloucestershire, Taunton, Jun 1949

131 consecutive dot balls
R. G. Nadkarni, India v. England, Madras, Jan 1964

137 consecutive dot balls
H. J. Tayfield, South Africa v. England, Durban, Jan 1957

80,000+ dot balls in a career
W. Rhodes (Yorks and England), 1898–1930
F. J. Titmus (Middx, Surrey and England), 1949–1982
C. W. L. Parker (Glos and England), 1903–1935

184,890 balls bowled in first-class career
W. Rhodes (Yorks and England), 1898–1930

*All 10 wickets for 25 at the age of 51 and after recovering from
a heart attack*
Roy Morley, Scholes v. Hatfield Town, 1980

61

All 20 wickets in a Test taken by bowlers whose surnames begin with letter B
R. G. Barlow (4 wkts), W. Barnes (2 wkts) and W. Bates (14 wkts), England v. Australia, Melbourne, Jan 1883

All 20 wickets in a Test taken by bowlers whose surnames begin with letter C
B. L. Cairns (10 wkts), E. J. Chatfield (6 wkts) and J. V. Coney (4 wkts), New Zealand v. England, Headingley, Jul 1983

All 20 wickets in a Test taken by bowlers whose surnames begin with letter L
J. C. Laker (19 wkts) and G. A. R. Lock (1 wkt), England v. Australia, Old Trafford, Jul 1956

Ball bowled into batsman's trouser pocket
P. D. Waters, Shell House v. Tunbridge Wells, 14 Jul 1949

Bail sent 67 yards 6 inches
by R. D. Burrows (Worcs) bowling W. Huddleston (Lancs), Old Trafford, 29 Jun 1911

Bail sent 66 yards 0 inches
by H. Larwood (MCC) bowling G. W. Martin (Tasmania), Launceston, 19 Jan 1929

Bail sent 64 yards 6 inches
by R. D. Burrows (Worcs) bowling A. C. MacLaren (Lancs), Old Trafford, 13 May 1901

Bail sent 63 yards 6 inches
by A. Mold (Lancs) bowling G. A. Lohmann (Surrey), The Oval, 20 Aug 1896

Bail sent 55 yards 1 foot
by W. Hitch (Surrey) bowling A. R. Tanner (Middx), The Oval, 18 Jul 1921

Bail sent 50 yards, and stump broken
by W. Bestwick (Derbys) bowling A. E. Thomas (Northants), Derby, 9 Jul 1921

Bowlers called for throwing in a Test match include
E. Jones Australia v. England, Melbourne, 1898
G. A. R. Lock England v. West Indies, Kingston, 1954
G. Griffin South Africa v. England, Lord's, 1960
Haseeb Ahsan Pakistan v. India, Bombay, 1960

I. Meckiff Australia v. South Africa, Brisbane, 1963
Abid Ali India v. New Zealand, Christchurch, 1968
S. M. H. Kirmani India v. West Indies, Bridgetown, 1983
D. I. Gower England v. New Zealand, Nottingham, 1986

Double century and a hat-trick in one match
W. E. Roller (204 and 6-44 including hat-trick), Surrey v.
Sussex, The Oval, 1885
Grant LeHuray, aged 14 (267* and 7-24 including hat-trick),
for Croydon Park, Sydney, 1948

Hat-trick spread over three seasons
Jed Bowers (Trevose, Cornwall), 1989–91

Nine men in the slip cordon
for D. K. Lillee (Aus) v. New Zealand, Christchurch, Feb 1977

Three hat-tricks in an innings by one bowler
M. F. McConnell Laxton House v. Bramston House, Oundle,
27 Jun 1939
W. Clarke St Augustine's College v. Ashford Church Choir,
Jun 1912
(Clarke also did the hat-trick twice in the second innings)

Worst analysis in Test cricket: 87-11-298-1
L. O'B. Fleetwood-Smith Australia v. England, The Oval, Aug
1938

CAPTAINS,

5

BATS AND BALLS

A winning captain is certainly a valuable asset to any cricket team. Sir Stanley Jackson, when just plain the Hon. F. S., won the toss five times out of five for England against Australia in 1905, the first time any man had been that lucky, and England won the series 2–0. It could not have been anything to do with his star sign, as both Jackson and his opposing captain Joe Darling were born on the same day, 21 November 1870.

Worcestershire in 1980 clearly thought that captaincy was no big deal. For their rain-affected Benson and Hedges semi-final tie against Essex at Worcester, which finally ended on 27 June, they were led by their official county captain that year, Norman Gifford. The next day, a Saturday, they decamped to Northampton for a county championship match. There they were captained by Glenn Turner. After one day's play in that match, they switched gears for a John Player League match, also against Northamptonshire at Northampton. This time they were led by somebody else again – their footballing cricketer, Ted Hemsley. Three captains in three days in three different competitions is a record that has never been matched. None of the three was particularly successful. Gifford led his team to defeat by eight wickets, Turner sat out most of a rain-affected draw, and Hemsley's team were beaten by seven wickets.

H. E. 'Tom' Dollery and J. R. Burnet share a remarkable distinction. They are the only men to have led both their county's first and second elevens to their respective championships. Dollery led Warwickshire to the County Championship in 1951, and in the twilight of his cricket career, led Warwickshire II to the Minor Counties title in 1959. Ronnie Burnet led Yorkshire II to the Minor Counties title in 1957, and then took over at the helm of the first team, to lead them to the Championship in 1959.

Some captains have resorted to unusual tactics in an attempt to win. Six runs were needed to win off the last ball of the Third Final Match of a Benson and Hedges World Series Cup between Australia and New Zealand at Melbourne on 1 February 1981, and with the final series tied at one match all, it was crucial to Australia that the New Zealand No. 10, Brian McKechnie, did not hit the ball out of the ground. So Australia's captain, Greg Chappell, instructed the bowler, his brother Trevor, to bowl underarm. This he did, and McKechnie, unable to hit the ball in the air, played it gently back to the bowler, and Australia won the series. The incident prompted many acid New Zealand comments about the new underarm deodorant, 'called Chappell and it stinks', but the delivery had been within the letter of the law if not the spirit.

A similar incident happened in a 1979 match between the Sussex League and the Southern League, when 18 runs were needed off two balls, apparently an impossibility. But the Southern League batsman hit the fifth ball of the over for six, and then the bowler bowled a no-ball. This too was hit over the ropes, so with six to win off the last ball, the Sussex League bowler reverted to what used to be officially described as a lob, but was probably more of a daisy-cutter.

Brian Rose, captain of Somerset, declared his team's innings closed at 1 for 0 against Worcestershire in a Benson and Hedges Cup zonal match on 24 May 1979, in order to maintain his team's striking rate and thus qualify for the quarter-final. Worcestershire won by ten wickets, of course, which meant that both teams qualified for the next stage. However, the TCCB met at Lord's a week later, and Somerset were disqualified for bringing the game into disrepute. This motion was passed by 17 votes to one, the one vote coming, curiously, not from Somerset but from Derbyshire.

Captaincy is often a talking-point in the Benson and Hedges Cup. In 1984, the Final was won by Lancashire, who beat Warwickshire by six wickets. The Gold Award winner was not Paul Allott (3 wickets for 15), or Steve Jefferies (3 for 28) or even Alvin Kallicharran for his superb 70 in a losing cause. Adjudicator Peter May gave the Gold Award to Lancashire captain John Abrahams, who made 0 and did not bowl. As *Wisden* cryptically remarked, the Award was 'as much for the part he had played in taking Lancashire to the Final as for any outstanding contribution on the day'. It would be entirely unfair to suggest that as he made no outstanding contribution on the day, what

Wisden are saying in effect is that he played no significant part in getting to the Final either.

Cricket equipment does not always survive the match. When Dennis Lillee began to champion an aluminium bat, he no doubt thought that one of the main advantages would be its long life. When he used it in a Test match, the first of the three-Test series against England at Perth in December 1979, the England captain Mike Brearley objected on the grounds that the ball was being scarred by contact with the metal bat. A vigorous discussion then took place, which ended with Lillee throwing the bat away, and finishing his innings with the more standard willow weapon. In the second innings, Lillee, batting woodenly throughout, was out 'c. Willey b. Dilley 19', a scoreline that the poets among the cricket reporters and their sub-editors had been waiting for since the touring team was announced.

Thomas 'Shock' White of Reigate turned up at a match between the Chertsey Club with Four Given Men against

67

the Hambledon Club at Laleham Burway on 23 September 1771 with a bat wider than the wicket. He had apparently used it in July that year to score a total of 197 runs in his two innings for Kent And Surrey against Middlesex And Hampshire at Sevenoaks, so word of his outsize weapon had gone before him. Even though Hambledon won the match against Chertsey by one run, despite the best efforts of one of its Given Men, the inevitable result of White's shock horror bat was that the rulers of cricket, then at Hambledon, decreed that the maximum breadth for a bat should be four and one quarter inches. All the same, 220 years later, during the match between the West Indian Board XI and the touring Australians in April 1991, Keith Arthurton was found to have a bat that was too wide, and had to change it.

Cricket bats are regularly broken, of course, but from time to time the ball itself has split apart under the most crucial circumstances. The *Auckland Star* on 12 April 1922 reported that during a match at Ti-Tree Point, one side had lost nine wickets, and needed a further two runs to

win. The batsman hit the ball high into the air, and 'lo and behold the ball broke apart into two halves in the air'. A fielder tried to catch one half as it tumbled to earth, but dropped it. However, he quickly picked up the demi-ball and threw the wicket down while the batsman was still well out of his crease going for the winning run. Appeals rent the air, but the umpire, quite correctly, said not out, as the ball was dead as soon as it split in two. The ball, and the score off it, were not counted, and the match resumed with one side still needing two to win, and the other with just one wicket to capture. The *Auckland Star* then ends its report, so we never learn who won.

A very similar event happened in Hong Kong in 1964. This time we know the teams involved, namely the Diocesan Boys School and the Kowloon Cricket Club Crusaders. Mr Turner, the Crusaders' captain, seemed to have snatched victory for his side when he took 16 runs off the first four balls of an over from an unnamed bowler (I suspect the bowler pleaded to remain anonymous), so that only three more runs were needed for victory. The fifth ball was belted by Turner, but by the most staggering coincidence, the reporter at the scene, one A. Porter, used exactly the same words as the *Auckland Star* to describe what happened next. 'Lo and behold,' wrote Mr Porter, using the time-honoured phrase for describing dis-integrating balls, 'the ball split'. The cork went for six, but the cover was caught by one of the fieldsmen. The Diocesan Boys started walking off, thinking the match was lost, but the cricketers in Hong Kong are as sharp

69

and as correct as the officials at Ti-Tree Point. One of the Crusaders, 'who had recently passed an umpire's exam', explained that the ball was dead as soon as it exhibited signs of terminal schizophrenia, so they went back on to the field to replay the fifth ball. This time, Mr Turner was caught behind, and the Diocesan Boys won by two runs.

In Bridgetown, Barbados, in 1894–95, the ball did not split. It disappeared. H. A. F. Cole, batting for Barbados against R. S. Lucas's XI, hit a ball from H. R. Bromley-Davenport towards the boundary, where it disappeared into a hole. It was never found.

70

OVERTHROWS

Chewing gum used to keep bails on
by Western Australia, at Perth, Dec 1952

Clay used to keep bails on
Australians v. Eleven Players of England, Harrogate, Sep 1902

Fielding side played in suits and overcoats
Nottinghamshire v. Hampshire, Southampton, 23 May 1930

Fielding side played in civvies because dressing room flooded in heavy rain
Derbyshire v. Yorkshire, Dewsbury, 10 Jun 1899

Iron bails used, in teeth of fierce wind
at Scarborough, 1869

Match played without bails, owing to gale
at Bootle, 1865

Old stumps used by parrot to sharpen beak
at Honley CC, 1980s

Rubber bails used by Essex
at Leyton, 1901

FAMILY
CONNECTIONS

Cricket is the aristocrat of sports, and the sport of aristocrats. In 1300 Edward I paid John Leek, a monk, the sum of £6.0.0 to coach his son Prince Edward at 'creag', which was probably an early form of cricket. HRH the Duke of Edinburgh has been President of the MCC on two separate occasions, and Prince Frederick, Prince of Wales, was the first member of the royal family to be killed by a cricket ball. This melancholy event occurred in 1751. *Wisden* notes only that in that year 'Prince Frederick took an interest in cricket'.

HM King George VI merited an obituary in *Wisden*, which read in part: 'When Prince Albert, he performed the hat-trick on the private ground on the slopes below

Windsor Castle, where the sons and grandsons of King Edward VII used to play regularly. A left-handed batsman and bowler, the king bowled King Edward VII, King George V and the present Duke of Windsor in three consecutive balls.' This is certainly the only time in history in which a future King of England and Emperor of India has bowled his three immediate predecessors with consecutive balls, even with the help of a sloping pitch.

72

King Edward VII was not a great cricketer, despite his patronage of the game. In 1863, when Prince of Wales, he was bowled first ball in a match in Ireland. His brother, Alfred, Duke of Edinburgh, was a better player, opening the batting for the Officers and Men of the Royal Yacht against the Royal Household in the 1860s. Leopold Duke of Albany was the scorer in this match.

The best European royal cricketer (always excepting the eight-year-old Prince Henry, Duke of Gloucester, who scored 250 in a single-wicket game at Frogmore in 1908 with his sister Mary (aged 11), later Princess Royal) was Edward VII's nephew Prince Christian Victor, elder son of Prince Christian of Schleswig Holstein. Christian Victor played one first-class game, for I Zingari against the Gentlemen of England at Scarborough on 29, 30 and 31 August 1887, scoring 35 in the first innings and a less wholesome 0 in the second. He remains the only royal cricketer to have played in a first-class match. Alongside him on the I Zingari side were two members of the nobility who were also Test cricketers, the Hon. M. B. Hawke, later Lord Hawke, and the Hon. Alfred Lyttelton. Almost exactly twenty years earlier, on August 26 1867,

Lyttelton had played for his family team against Bromsgrove School. The school scored 150, but the Lytteltons had set them 214 to win, and thus won by 63 runs with what must surely be the most ermine-ridden eleven ever to play an organized game of cricket. In batting order, they were Lord Lyttelton, the Hon. C. G. Lyttelton, the Hon. A. V. Lyttelton, the Hon. N. G. Lyttelton, the Hon. S. G. Lyttelton, the Hon. A. T. Lyttelton, the Hon. R. H. Lyttelton, the Hon. E. Lyttelton, the Hon. A. Lyttelton, the Hon. and Rev. W. H. Lyttelton and the Hon. Spencer Lyttelton.

73

On the Commonwealth team's tour of India and Ceylon in 1950–51, their opponents included no fewer than seven members of the Indian nobility. Against Saurashtra, they faced Thakore Saheb of Rajkot, who top-scored with 29 in Saurashtra's first innings; in the next game, Baroda included the Yuvaraja of Baroda at No. 6; Patiala fielded not only their Maharaja but also the Raja of Nalagiri; the Maharajah of Patiala played again for the Bombay Governor's XI, along with the 72-year-old Raja Maharaj Singh; the Raja of Jath played for his own eleven in the Commonwealth's next game, but made only 3; and the Maharajah of Bhavnagar, playing for the Madras Governor's XI, had the honour of being bowled by Sonny Ramadhin in both innings.

The most successful Indian princes in cricket, however, were Kumar Shri Ranjitsinhji, HH Jam Saheb of Nawanagar, who scored 72 first-class centuries and played for England 15 times; his nephew Duleepsinhji, who was educated at Cheltenham College and was only prevented by ill health from emulating some of his uncle's achievements; and the father and son Nawabs of Pataudi, both of whom captained India in Test cricket. The son, later known as Mansur Ali Khan, matched Ranjitsinhji when he lost the use of an eye. Pataudi lost his in a car crash, Ranji in a shooting accident.

Sir Gajapatairaj Vijaya Ananda, the Maharajkumar of Vizianagram, known as Vizzy, also captained India and became the first knight to play in a Test match when he played in the second Test against England, at Old Trafford on 25 July 1936. He had been knighted between the First and Second Tests. Only Sir Richard Hadlee of New Zealand has subsequently played Test cricket after having been knighted.

Thebaw, King of Burma, was a keen cricketer while a student at Dr Marles' Missionary School in Mandalay from 1869. The reverend doctor, writing about his royal pupil's cricketing ability, reported that he 'batted fairly well, but refused to do his share of the fielding, and was in the habit of using very injurious language to anyone who bowled him'. He sounds like a typical village cricketer, for all his royal birth.

King Hussein of Jordan, who was educated at Harrow, showed much better sportsmanship when he played for the Royal Amman Cricket Club against the British Embassy in 1971. His contribution is not recorded, but the result is. The Royal Amman Cricket Club won, another triumph for British diplomacy.

In 1907, a Fijian cricket team toured Australia, under the captaincy of Prince Penaia Kadavulevu Thakombau, grandson of King Thakombau who ceded the Fiji Islands to the British throne in 1874. In 1880, King George V, then Prince George and a cadet on board HMS *Bacchante*, played cricket in Lekuva, Fiji, but 'it was reported that the Prince's innings did not greatly affect the total'.

Even the only marginally blue-blooded enjoy their cricket, but love of the game seems to be hereditary. Family links in the game are among the most widely researched and speculated upon in all sports journalism. Oxford and Cambridge Universities have, for almost two hundred years, been a depository of the well connected if not particularly well educated, and the list of men who have won Blues at cricket reads like the membership of a hundred Hunt Ball Committees. A wonderful book called *Oxford v. Cambridge at the Wicket* by F. S. Ashley-Cooper and Sir Pelham Warner, first published in 1926, delights in genealogical asides. A footnote to the 1902 game states that 'M. Bonham-Carter's mother was sister of C. L. and F. H. Norman. He was thus connected with the Nepean, Jenner, Dyke, Wathen and Barnard families (see genealogical table facing page 249 in *The History of*

Kent County Cricket).' The comment on the 1921 match was that 'there was no close relationship between W. G. L. F. Lowndes, of this year's Oxford team, and R. Lowndes who took part in the match of 1841; but the whole Lowndes family are all more or less connected.'

On 2 July 1992, the Crawley brothers John and Mark both scored centuries for different first-class teams on the same day. John hit 106 not out as he led Cambridge University to a seven-wicket victory over Oxford at Lord's, while elder brother Mark hit his hundred for Nottinghamshire against Kent at Maidstone. In 1989 Robin and Chris Smith had also scored centuries for different teams on the same day, 27 July. Robin scored 143 for England against Australia at Old Trafford, his first Test century, and elder brother Chris scored 107 for Hampshire against Gloucestershire at Portsmouth.

In the University match of 1919, F. W. Gilligan and F. C. G. Naumann played for Oxford, while their respective brothers, A. E. R. Gilligan and J. H. Naumann, played for Cambridge. A. E. R. Gilligan was stumped by his brother F. W. in Cambridge's first innings, and J. H. Naumann was clean bowled by his brother in Cambridge's second innings. With this fraternal domination by the Oxonian pair, it is not surprising that Oxford won by 45 runs.

Two brothers ganged up on a third in the Middlesex v. Somerset match at Lord's in June 1933. H. W. Lee of Middlesex was 'c. F. S. Lee b. J. W. Lee 82' in the most fratricidal dismissal yet recorded in first-class cricket.

During the Derbyshire v. Warwickshire match at Derby

on 3 and 5 June, 1922, W. G. Quaife (aged 50) and his son Bernard (aged 22) were batting together for a time against the bowling of two generations of Derbyshire pace, R. S. Bestwick (aged 22) and his far more successful father Billy (aged 47). This event is unique in first-class cricket, but commonplace enough in village matches. Three generations played for Denchworth and Charney CC in 1976. E. J. Clarke, aged 55, and his grandson D. Terry, aged 12, were the extreme ends of this genealogical curiosity, with Clarke's son-in-law, young D. Terry's dad, also in the eleven.

77

Sussex is the county for family connections. Against Warwickshire on 7, 8 and 9 June 1939, three pairs of brothers played in the side. James and John Langridge, Jim and Harry Parks and Charles and Jack Oakes all took part in the match at Horsham, which Sussex won by four wickets. Two unrelated players called Cornford were also in the Sussex side, leaving only Mr H. T. Bartlett, H. E. Hammond and J. Nye without namesakes. Jack Oakes, incidentally, rejoiced in the middle name of Ypres, the only first-class cricketer to be named after a First World War battle.

Five brothers once took part in a first-class match together, but three played on one side, and two on the other. On 14, 15, 16 and 17 December 1961, the semi-final of the Quaid-I-Azam Trophy between the Karachi Whites and the Karachi Blues included Raees, Hanif and Mushtaq Mohammad playing for the Whites, and Wazir and Sadiq Mohammad playing for the Blues. Although four of the five were Test cricketers (Raees being the odd one out, only making it to twelfth man for Pakistan), no more than three of the brothers ever played together for their country.

Four Newhall brothers, George, Daniel, Robert and Charles, played for the United States against Canada in September 1880, the largest fraternal gathering in any international side. Four members of the Ayling family played for the North of Argentina against the South of Argentina at Belgrano in 1939. Dennet Ayling made 256*, the highest score ever made in Argentina.

Full family elevens are not uncommon. From the Colmans of Norfolk (the mustard people) who put out eleven brothers in one team in the 1840s, to another Norfolk family, the Edriches, who in 1947 were as strong as most county sides, the appearance of teams of eleven good men and true, all with the same surname, has become so regular in Britain as to be scarcely a curiosity.

In Denmark, it is a different matter. The Morild family of Jutland were for many years the backbone of the Danish national side. When Thomas Morild celebrated his sixtieth birthday in 1947, the Morild family challenged the rest of Denmark to a match, and won.

The Trant family have reason to be fed up with Mark Page of Sholing Ramblers CC. In June 1988, Page achieved a hat-trick for his team, dismissing first Tim Trant, then Simon Trant, and finally Patrick Trant. All three brothers were bowled by balls which hit their off stump. The Mundin family had two hat-tricks to celebrate on the same day in 1987, when father Brian took three wickets in three balls for his South Lakeland League Club, Ibis, while his 14-year-old son Phillip repeated the performance for his school team.

The Foxon brothers combined for a remarkable hat-trick in 1979, while playing for Hinckley CC Under-15s. The first batsman was caught by 13-year-old Richard Foxon off his 15-year-old brother Peter's bowling. Next ball, 10-year-old Stephen Foxon stumped the new batsman, and Peter completed the hat-trick by clean bowling his man next ball. Their father was standing as square-leg umpire.

79

ENTIRE FAMILY ELEVENS

Buckingham	v. Maltravers at Huish Champflower, 1984
Christopherson	'on more than one occasion', 1887–91
Colman	regularly in Norfolk, 1840s
Duckering	v. H. T. Hurst's XI, 1882
Edrich	regularly in Norfolk, 1940s on
Garnett	v. Western Club at Eccles, 1872
Maltravers	v. Buckingham at Huish Champflower, 1984
Partridge (with 6 reserves)	v. Birdlip & Brimpsfield, 1983
Snowdon	v. Callington, 1978
Thompson	v. Sydney Stock Exchange at Rushcutter's Bay, 1893
Veivers	in Queensland, Australia, 1950s

YOUNG, OLD AND ODDLY NAMED

7

There are many claimants to the title of Oldest Cricketer. Among the oldest successful cricketers is 73-year-old Jack Cleaver, who took 9 for 45 for Leicestershire's Glenfrith CC against Hallaton in 1986. This was not, however, his best ever bowling analysis, as he had taken all ten in 1929, 57 years earlier. Probably the oldest cricketer ever to play regularly at any organized level was Mr Frederick Lester of Yoxall, Staffordshire. In 1957, it was reported that he was still playing for the village at the age of 87. He was for a while on the injured list, having hurt his back gardening, and although his sons Frederick, aged 67, and Christopher, 64, had already retired from cricket, Mr Lester senior firmly intended to carry on playing.

Charles Absolon, the London club cricketer of the last century, claimed to have taken 209 wickets in 1893, when he was 76 years old. In 1897, at the age of 80, he obtained 100 wickets. He did the hat-trick 59 times after the age of 54, during which time he also took well over 6,000 wickets. He was less agile as a batsman, and, as *Wisden* records, 'during his last few years, he employed the services of a runner'. Rather less spectacular than Mr Absolon, but still very impressive, is the performance of Dick Tolkein of Warlingham CC, who from his sixtieth birthday in 1971 until the end of the decade took 572 wickets for his club. Jack Watson, of Bearpark CC, County Durham, did the hat-trick in May 1991 at the age of 70.

In 1907, at the age of 65, Dr E. M. Grace, W. G.'s elder brother, claimed to have taken 212 wickets in the season for Thornbury, and to have had 208 catches missed off his bowling. He was likely to have been as certain of the total of missed catches as of the wickets taken, such was the competitiveness of the Grace family.

The oldest man to appear in a first-class game is the Raja Maharaj Singh, who was reputed to be 72 years old when he captained the Bombay Governor's XI against the Commonwealth touring team at Bombay on 25, 26 and 27 November 1950. He batted at No. 9, and made 4 out of the Governor's XI first innings total of 202 before being 'c. Emmett b. Laker'. He thus became undoubtedly the great Surrey off-spinner's oldest first-class victim, and quite probably the only one born in the nineteenth century. Laker was 44 years younger than his victim, and this is almost certainly the greatest age gap between bowler and victim in first-class cricket history. The Raja was not one of the eight bowlers used as the Commonwealth piled up 483 for 5 in reply, and in the Governor's second innings, he was listed as 'absent ill'. His side went down to defeat by an innings and 173 runs.

The oldest player to turn out in a County Championship match was also making his debut for the county, although he had many years before played for Oxford University and Lancashire. This was the Rev Reginald Moss, who was born on 24 February 1868, and played one match for Worcestershire, against Gloucestershire at Worcester from 23 to 26 May 1925, when he was 57 years old. He made 2 in the first innings before falling caught and bowled by C. W. L. Parker. In the second innings he was bowled for 0 by an even greater Gloucestershire player, Walter Hammond, who was over 35 years younger than his victim. Moss had played for Oxford against Cambridge 14 years before Hammond was born.

On Monday 13 August 1838, there was a match on the Hyde Park Ground in Sheffield between the Town of Sheffield and The Surrounding Villages. It was a 16-a-side game, and all the players on either side were over the age of sixty. The *Sheffield Independent* reported that 'the game was played in quite the old style; there were slow bowling, and the blocking, snipping and on-hitting which our fathers have seen exhibited in many a well contested match.'

The oldest man to have umpired a match at Lord's is Joseph W. Filliston. He was 100 years old when he stood in the Lord's Taverners v. Old England match in 1962, and died in 1964, aged 102, having been knocked down by a motor scooter. Also 102 when he died was John Wheatley, who played for Canterbury, New Zealand, between 1882 and 1904. He finally lost his bails to the Great Stumper in the Sky on 20 April 1962, but his Life's Great Innings had been the longest ever recorded by a first-class cricketer.

83

The youngest cricketer to have scored a century is a record equally hard fought over. Graeme Hick is reputed to have scored his first hundred at the age of seven, and Gregor MacGregor, England's wicketkeeper in the 1890s, claimed to have scored three hundreds at the age of nine. Percy Chapman hit 102 at the age of 12 for Oakham Under-14s, the same age at which Donald Bradman, playing for Bowral High School against Mittagong School, scored 115 not out in a total of 156, which he describes as 'my first century'. But young centurions are becoming commonplace. Left-handed opening bat Michael Brown, aged 10, hit 149 not out for Lancashire

Under-11s against Kent Under-11s on 1 August 1991, the highest score ever made in the Under-11 Schools Festival, but it was the sixth century in all inter-county matches at that Festival.

The youngest player to score a hundred in a Test match is Mushtaq Mohammed of Pakistan, who was 17 years and 82 days old when he scored 101 against India at New Delhi on 12 February 1961. The oldest man to score a Test century is Jack Hobbs, of Surrey and England, who was exactly 29 years older than Mushtaq, at 46 years and 82 days, when he completed his fifteenth and final Test century at Melbourne on 8 March 1929.

Many cricketers have had long careers. Private Sadler first played for the RASC on 20 June 1931. In his first two-innings match, he was dismissed by Oliver Battcock in both innings, although in the first innings he was well past his 50 when he was 'c. Ambler b. Battcock'. Thirty years later, on 2 and 3 September 1961, Major L. A. J. Sadler played his final match for the Corps. In this game he was also dismissed by the same Oliver Battcock in

both innings. Battcock, an actor and producer whose stage name was Oliver Gordon, took over 6,000 wickets in a career which lasted over fifty years, playing for Buckinghamshire, Datchet, Thespids, Cryptics, XL Club and the Incogniti among others, so perhaps it is not surprising that he was better known as a cricketer than as an actor.

When I played for my college in the sixties, I often batted in tandem with a fellow student called Ray Currie. We were the regular last-wicket pair, and it amused our opponents that, despite being called Currie and Rice, we never got the runs. Names of cricketers occasionally amuse and often confuse players, spectators and statisticians alike. 'Caught Beet bowled Root' was a common scoreline for teams playing Derbyshire in the years before the First World War, when Fred Root and George Beet were both county regulars, but the equally rustic A. W. Oates and A. B. Wheat never played together for Nottinghamshire, despite both being in and out of the county side between 1931 and 1933.

There have been many cricketers with generally appropriate cricketing names. A. Fielder played for Kent in the early years of this century; Peter Bowler is an opening batsman for Derbyshire. While no Batter has played top level cricket, there have been Ron Hooker (Middlesex), Geoff Pullar (Lancashire, Gloucestershire and England), P. J. Hacker (Nottinghamshire), S. A. Block (Surrey), Lt. S. F. Edge (Blackpool CC) and G. N. Duck (Gentlemen of Yorkshire). J. W. Seamer (Somerset), F. J. Pitcher

(Victoria), A.E. Dipper (Gloucestershire), T. Shooter (Nottinghamshire) and Brian Lobb (Somerset) add variety to our bowling names, as does I.W. Quick, who most inconveniently bowled slow-left-arm spin for Victoria. H.W. Game played for Gloucestershire in 1884, and F.W. Sides played for Victoria. R.I. Scorer (Worcestershire) is there, but there is no Umpire. We have to make do with E.W. Bastard (Oxford University and Somerset). The Clapps, A.E. and R.J. of Somerset, will provide sound effects.

There's a full cricket bag of equipment among cricketers' names, too. J.W. Box kept wicket for Middlesex, J. Boot played for Derbyshire in 1895, and Balls have played for Gloucestershire, Northamptonshire and Somerset among others. Four Studds played for Middlesex, and P.A.C. Bail was a Cambridge Blue in 1986, 1987 and 1988. Then there is W.L.C. Creese (Hampshire), A. Chance (Shrewsbury), and C.H. Cort (Warwickshire). E. Capp played for New South Wales a century ago.

Speaking of caps, it is worth recording in passing the effect that the award of a county cap can have. Before Surrey's Refuge Assurance League match against Warwickshire at The Oval on 8 July 1990, Surrey's Darren Bicknell, Chris Bullen and David Ward were all awarded their county caps. All three then went out and made ducks to show they were worth their caps, as did Darren Bicknell's already-capped brother Martin, as a mark of family solidarity. Despite these four ducks, the seven who did score made enough runs to take Surrey to victory by 15 runs.

In order to transport all these cricketing names from match to match, we could use a Carr (D. B. of Derbyshire or his son J. of Middlesex), E. Coupe and R. T. deVille (both Derbyshire), and the various necessary parts such as a Boot, a Fender (P. G. H. of Surrey), a Horne, a spare Wheal but with any luck no Dent (C. H.). If we are still Carless (E., Glamorgan 1934 to 1936), we can always take the Buss.

Tony Buss of Sussex took a wicket with his second ball in county cricket, when he clean bowled W. E. Jones of Glamorgan, at Pontypridd on 30 July 1958. Jones thus became the first county cricketer to miss A. Buss. The first player to catch A. Buss was R. L. Jowett of Oxford University. The scoreboard on 18 June 1958 read 'A Buss, c. Jowett b. Raybould 15'. His brother Mike Buss also played for Sussex with him, which was typical. After having no Busses in the Sussex side for over eighty years, suddenly two come along at once.

Tony Buss also lived through two astonishing near misses when batting for Sussex against Yorkshire at Bradford in May 1965. In the first innings, he missed a ball from Tony Nicholson, which hit the off stump, but the bail jammed between the off and middle stumps without falling to the ground. The ball went for four byes. In the second innings he hit a ball from Chris Balderstone on to his foot and then on to the stumps. Again, a bail was dislodged, but did not fall to the ground. As Buss was 5 not out at the end of the match, which was drawn because Yorkshire could not capture the final Sussex wicket before time ran out, the two let-offs for Buss were just the ticket.

Probably the longest name ever given to a serious cricketer is that of the Fijian cricketer of the 1950s and 1960s, who was called Ilikena Lasurusa Talebulamaine-iilikenamainavaleniveivakabulaimainakulalakebalau, a surname of 62 letters. This name roughly means 'returned alive from Nakula Hospital at Lakemba island in the Lau Group'. Fortunately for scorers around the South Pacific, he shortened his name to 'I. L. Bula' for cricketing purposes.

When W. H. Denton opened the batting for Northamptonshire with his brother J. S. Denton against Somerset at Northampton on 24 June 1914, they were helping to establish a record which all scorers and commentators hope will never be equalled, or worse still, beaten. William and John Denton were identical twins, who caused tremendous confusion for everybody when they batted together, to say nothing of their efforts in the field which were often wrongly attributed. But on this particular day, the Dentons were not the only problem. The Somerset innings was opened by the twins Albert and Arthur Rippon. According to the official scorecards, John Denton

made 12 and William Denton made 74 in helping Northamptonshire to a commanding total of 410. In reply
Albert Rippon made 0 and Arthur 1 as Somerset tumbled
to 123, and had to follow on. In the second innings Albert
managed 11 and Arthur 32, as Somerset lost by an innings.
Perhaps understanding the scorers' problems, neither
Denton bowled or took a catch during the entire game.

Arthur Rippon's attempt to baffle the scorers continued
after the Great War. He is probably the only cricketer to
have played first-class cricket under an assumed name.
Playing for Somerset against Gloucestershire on 9 and 10
June 1919, he was listed on the scorecard as 'S. Trimnell'.
No explanation is given for this extraordinary occurrence,
and his nom-de-bat fooled nobody. His twin Albert was
also playing, so everybody must have noticed the resem-
blance, and *Wisden*, in its report the following year,
merely states laconically, 'A.E.S. Rippon, who played
under an assumed name, enjoyed by far his biggest success
during the season'. He made 92 and 58 not out, as
Somerset won by seven wickets.

HOME AND AWAY

The setting of a cricket match is part of the match itself. Cricket grounds, from English village greens to the Gaddafi Stadium, Lahore, all have their own personality and all affect the way cricket is played. Cricket has been played all over the world, from Antarctica to the North Pole, and from the Himalayas to the Goodwin Sands. Not all grounds are as grand as Lord's or as massive as the Melbourne Cricket Ground, but the eccentricity of cricket and of cricketers is no respecter of time or place.

The ground at Baldon Green in Oxfordshire has a road running through it. If the ball is hit towards the pavilion, a humble structure which stands beyond the midwicket boundary, the chasing fielders have to stop at the edge of

the road, look left, look right and left again, before continuing their pursuit of the 'crimson rambler', which by now will have rolled over the boundary. There is a tree on the boundary at Ynysygerwn CC which has been painted white to act as a sightscreen.

The old gold mining town of Walhalla in Victoria, Australia, had a cricket pitch on the top of a hill. The miners had blasted the top off the hill to make a flat ground big enough to play cricket on. There were two approaches to the ground, one a gentle but fairly long walk up, the other a very steep and difficult climb. When Walhalla CC had a home game, the home side were in the habit of taking the gentle route up on the night before the game, and camping at the top. Visiting teams were not usually told about the easy route, nor about the advisability of getting there the night before, so they would arrive at the foot of a precipice, up which they had to carry not only themselves but also their cricket bags. Even teams that arrived in time for the start were in no fit state to play well. Most teams never got there until the home side had claimed the toss. No fielders at Walhalla ever chased the ball beyond the edge of the playing area. Walhalla is now a ghost town, so the climb up the hill is no longer made by Australians carrying cricket bags, only by tourists with cameras.

Another mining team had to give up using their ground for a quite different reason. The South Crofty Tin Mine XI were banned by Kerrier District Council from using their ground at Roskear in Cornwall in 1988, after 18 years of playing there, because big hitting had broken too many windows on the nearby housing estate. It was not made clear whether the big hitters were playing for South Crofty or for their opponents, but South Crofty got the blame.

If only there had been a new motorway built near Roskear, the problem might have been solved. Epping Foresters CC celebrated the reopening of their ground on 12 May 1986. The ground was relaid over the tunnel roof of the London orbital M25 motorway, and now the only windows in danger of being broken are those of the drivers hurtling in and out of the tunnel a few metres below.

In 1991, two nuclear submarines surfaced near the North Pole so that the crews could play cricket. HMS *Tireless* and USS *Pargo* managed to find a level ice floe, and they laid out a rope matting pitch. Despite this, the bowlers' run-ups and the outfield were treacherous. It was difficult to work out how many runs were scored, mainly because the crew of the USS *Pargo* had little idea of the Laws of cricket, but we know that an appeal

against the light was turned down on the quite reasonable grounds that the sun had not set for two months, and was unlikely to do so for several weeks to come. The crowd of about a hundred submariners and a few seals may have been cold, but they outnumbered the crowds to be seen on the Thursday morning of some county matches in England.

In 1822, there was a match played 'at Igloolik in the frozen North' between the crews of HMS *Fury* and HMS *Hecla*, but the result is unknown. Cricket was played under the midnight sun on an ice fjord at Spitzbergen by players including Alfred Shaw and Lord Sheffield in the late nineteenth century, and in 1969 a New Zealand side played matches at the South Pole. Bad light caused the cancellation of crew members' plans to play cricket at the North Pole, when the Royal Navy nuclear submarine *Sovereign* surfaced there in October 1976. In 1985, there were several games on the Bowden Neve Snowfield in Antarctica, during the Antarctic Treaty Conference.

Playing on ice has happened frequently. In the winter of 1889–90, Mr E. Hammond's XI played Mr H. Crowhurst's XV on ice at Storrington. The players all wore top hats. *Wisden's Cricketers' Almanac* of 1880 reports the terrible severity of the winter of 1878–79, which continued up to the middle of May 1879, 'and even then, the cold winds seemed loth to leave the land they had so sorely stricken with distress, disease and death'. However, as *Wisden* records, 'there is no black cloud without its silver lining, and one bright spot in this dark winter was that its severity and length enabled more CRICKET

MATCHES ON THE ICE.' On 17 December 1878, on the Duke of Devonshire's Swiss Cottage Pond, a seven-a-side match was played between members of the Sheffield Skating Club. Mr R. Gillott's side beat Mr B. Chatterton's side by eleven runs, Mr W. Shearstone top-scoring with 20 for the winning side. *Wisden* devotes five pages to recording a total of 12 matches on the ice, including one by moonlight on the night of 7 January 1879 on the ice in Windsor Great Park between Mr Bowditch's Side and Mr Gage's Side. The highest score of the winter was 105 by Mr D. Hearfield on 25 January 1879 on the ice at Partington Carrs for Mr L. W. Wallgate's Side against Mr C. Ullathorne's Side. The highest team score on ice was 326, by Cambridge Town against Cambridge University, in the three-day match on the ice at Grantchester on 17, 18 and 19 December 1878.

English teams have regularly played on ice on the frozen lake at St Moritz in Switzerland, under which David Gower also once parked his car.

Less satisfactory than ice as a cricketing surface is sand. Cricket, of a sort, has been played on Goodwin Sands, a few miles off the Kent coast, since at least the middle of the last century. It is a damp surface, not very level, and the ball does not tend to bounce very much. In fact, a cricket ball does not bounce at all, which is why a rubber ball is normally used. The outfield is very wet, and the most frequent complaint from the batsmen is of seals moving behind the bowler's arm. Matches are necessarily short, to beat the incoming tide, but that does not stop members of the Goodwin Sands Potholing Club from playing every year on their annual trip to the Sands. The full Kent county side also played there in 1989, for Chris Cowdrey's benefit. It is the only ground at which the pavilion is a hovercraft.

In Fiji, there is a ground at Waiyevo on the island of Taveuni, through which the 180° meridian passes. It is therefore theoretically possible to hit the ball on a Saturday, field it on a Sunday, and throw it back in to the previous Saturday. However, as the International Date Line is officially bent out to sea wherever it crosses land, it would take a mighty hit (and a fielder who was also a strong swimmer) actually to achieve this feat.

On 30 June 1927, Mr J. E. A. Bye, playing in the annual Aysgarth Schoolmasters v. The Borderers match, bowled a ball which pitched and then 'crept along the ground slowly and mysteriously'. On close investigation, it turned out that Mr Bye's delivery had landed on half an upturned fork, which fixed itself securely to the outer cover of the ball. The fork had obviously been left there by the groundsman and been pressed into the ground by the roller, because it had not been noticed during the careful preparation of the pitch during the previous weeks of the season. While Mr Bye and his fellow fielders were lost in amazement at this curiosity, the batsmen, appropriately enough, ran a leg bye.

The most famous case of difficulties with the pitch took place at Headingley in the early hours of Tuesday 19 August 1975, the final day of the Third Test between England and Australia. Four people got into the ground and under the covers at the pavilion end. There they dug holes near the popping crease and poured a gallon of crude oil across the wicket, on a length. The match had to be abandoned as a draw, though rain which set in at midday would probably have ended the game anyway. The reason for the sabotage was to plead the innocence of the convicted bank robber George Davis. The leader of the saboteurs, Peter Chappell, was sentenced to 18 months' imprisonment on 6 January at Birkenhead Crown Court, and he served 13 months of the sentence. The other villains of the piece were Colin Dean, Richard Ramsey and an American, Mrs Geraldine Hughes, who could not have been expected to understand what she was doing to the English psyche.

Vandals also destroyed the pitch at Portsmouth a year later. On the night of 13–14 June 1976, the pitch being used for the Hampshire v. Yorkshire game was partially dug up, and the match had to be moved to an adjoining wicket. In 1913, suffragettes decided that Tunbridge Wells pavilion was a symbol of the oppression of women, and burnt it to the ground.

The groundsman at the Parks, Oxford, found a tramp sleeping under the covers on Sunday 22 May 1988, the rest day of the match between the University and Lancashire. It was reported that 'a mysterious wet patch appeared on a good length', but this unauthorized watering of the wicket did not seem to worry Lancashire's batsmen. On the Monday they took their total from 19 for 0 to 429 for 7 declared.

One of the problems that any village cricketer can identify with is that of trying to find a ground for an away fixture. Mafi Khan, a Pakistani hoping for some cricket in Australia in the winter of 1988–89, arrived fifteen days late after his travel agent in Islamabad had booked him to Obock, Tanzania, instead of Hobart, Tasmania. However, Mafi should be thankful he was not a member of the 1882 Australian team which toured England. It was calculated that by the time they returned home they had travelled a total of 35,296 miles, or 882.4 miles for each of the forty matches they played on the tour.

One cricket ground you cannot miss is in India. In a local park near Ahmedabad, there is an unmissable tourist's delight in the form of a three-storey high concrete cricket bat, engraved with the names of India's 1972 Test side, and the signature of the captain, Ajit Wadekar. The team beat England 2–1 in the Test series that winter, the only time England were captained by Welshman Tony Lewis.

Travel can be a great problem for cricketers. Ken Howard of Lancashire missed his train one morning in June 1963, and thus was unable to continue his innings against Derbyshire at Liverpool. He was listed as 'retired out 1'. When Greg Ritchie and Wayne Phillips missed the team bus on the morning of the Australians' match against the Leeward Islands in 1984, two substitute fielders had to be found until the errant pair turned up. At Leyton in 1925, only two of the Surrey team turned up in time for the start of their day's play against Essex. Sportingly, the

Essex openers C. A. G. Russell and J. A. Cutmore made no attempt to score against the bowling of Percy Fender and A. Jeacocke until the coach with the rest of the Surrey side turned up, at 11.40 a.m. Surrey's wicketkeeper Bert Strudwick, who had padded up en route, ran on to the field of play to take over the gloves from Jeacocke, with the cry, 'How many byes?'

On Monday 17 June 1963, only three Middlesex players were on hand to resume their innings against Kent at Tunbridge Wells at 11.30. What was worse, one of the trio had been out already, on the Saturday evening, and another was the twelfth man. Only R. A. White, who had been not out 43 over the weekend, was ready and qualified to play. On an appeal from Kent, the umpires ordered Middlesex to close their innings, under Law 17, note 1 (iii) of the 1947 code then in operation, because Middlesex 'will not, or cannot, continue play'. White remained 'not out' for the statisticians, his overnight partner Ron Hooker was given out 'absent 13', and the rest of the team were credited with a 'did not bat' apiece. In the ten minutes allowed between innings, two more players, Don Bennett and John Price arrived, and twelfth man Clarke was given permission to keep wicket. All the same, Kent provided several substitutes, one of whom (Prodger) caught Kent's opener Brian Luckhurst off Bennett's bowling for 4 in the three overs which were bowled before the rest of the Middlesex team arrived at the ground. Rain set in the next day and the match ended in an uneventful draw.

'Rain stopped play' is the least curious of cricketing events, at least in England. 'Sun stopped play' is less usual. In June 1958, a Bradford League match between Bingley and Baildon had to be stopped as the sun was setting dead in line with the wicket. This reportedly caused six overs to be lost, although how they continued to play after the sun had successfully set was not explained.

Sunshine reflected off the windscreens of motor cars has become such a common problem at cricket matches that most people now cover their screens with blankets or the like if ever there is a risk of the sun breaking through during a day's cricket watching. Perhaps the earliest recorded instance of sunshine stopping play was at Hastings in early August 1938. Given the unlikelihood of sun coming out at any South Coast resort in August, the guilty motorist could be forgiven for his error, but it is interesting to note the remedy used in those more casual pre-war days. The players just stopped playing for ten minutes until the movement of the sun made the glare less obvious. These days the loudspeakers would have been working overtime, and ground staff would have been seeking out the villain with tracker dogs and Attack With Botham cricket bats.

An eclipse of the sun has only once prevented play in a Test match. The Golden Jubilee Test between India and England at the Wankhede Stadium, Bombay, in February 1980, ended in a victory for England by ten wickets, thanks mainly to Ian Botham, who clearly is at his most effective when the heavens conspire to create the right conditions. The second day of the match, 16

99

February, was declared a rest day because of the eclipse, but the Indian batsmen batted as though they were in a permanent penumbra against the swing bowling of Botham. He took 6 for 58 before the eclipse, and 7 for 48 after it, not to mention scoring 114 somewhere in between. This is a curiosity in itself, the first time one man has scored a century and taken 13 wickets in a Test.

On page 40 of the 1976 *Wisden Cricketers' Almanack* is testimony to the vagaries of the English summer. A photograph captioned 'a freak snow storm covers the ground' shows the conditions for the second day's play in the Derbyshire v. Lancashire match at Buxton, on 2 June 1975. While such severe conditions usually mean play is suspended, a match between George Parr's touring side and a United States team at Rochester, New York in October 1859 continued despite conditions so bad that the fielders played in muffs and greatcoats. During the MCC match against Oxford University in May 1893, the cold forced fielders to wear gloves and coats.

OVERTHROWS

Ball lost down a rabbit hole
at Falkirk, 1976

Batsman interrupting innings to conduct funeral
Rev Lancelot Smith v. Indian Students, at Spalding, 1926

Batsman interrupting innings to conduct wedding
Curate of Aylesbury, at Aylesbury, 1922

Bomb scare stops play for 89 minutes
England v. West Indies, Lord's, from 2.42 p.m., 25 Aug 1973

Cricket at the Olympics
Devon and Somerset County Wanderers (Britain) beat USFSA (France) by 158 runs, at Vélodrome de Vincennes, 19–20 Aug 1900

Fielder lighting fire in outfield at Blackpool
Arthur Coningham, Australians v. XVI of Blackpool and District, 1893

First cricket team to travel by air
Lancashire CCC, from Cardiff to Southampton, 26 Jul 1935

First match with broadcast commentary (by P. F., later Sir Pelham, Warner)
Essex v. New Zealanders, Leyton, 14 May 1927

First Sunday game at Lord's
Middlesex v. Lord's Taverners (12-a-side), 1 Aug 1965

Ground used by two different counties for home fixtures
Abbeydale Park, Sheffield by Derbyshire, 1946 and 1947
                              by Yorkshire, 1976
The Oval by Surrey as headquarters
          by Middlesex v. Nottinghamshire, 1939

Play suspended through lack of rain
Jersey, Aug 1949

Three Test matches played on the same day, for the first time
West Indies v. Australia at Port-of-Spain, Trinidad ⎫ 16 Mar
Pakistan v. England at Faisalabad   ⎬ 1984
Sri Lanka v. New Zealand at Colombo   ⎭

HOW OUT

9

Cricketers seem to have the knack of finding new ways of losing their wicket. Whatever the circumstances, however propitious the auguries for a big score, some batsmen just seem to know how to get themselves back to the pavilion more quickly than originally planned. Some batsmen don't even appear to try to score runs. James Southerton, who among other curiosities is the oldest man ever to make his Test debut, at the age of 49 years and 119 days, was recorded as being 'retired out, thinking he was caught' in a game for Surrey against MCC Club and Ground in 1870. Thomas Sidwell, the Leicestershire wicketkeeper, never even made it out on to the pitch. He was given out 'absent, lost on Tube' against Surrey at The Oval on 26 August 1921. He had been batting, with his score at 1 not out overnight, but

managed to get himself lost on the London underground in trying to make his way from the team's hotel to the ground the next morning. Surrey's captain, P. G. H. Fender refused to allow Sidwell to bat when he did finally turn up, and Leicestershire went on to lose the match by 88 runs. If Fender's action seems unsporting, it must be remembered that this was Surrey's final home match of the season, and their final fixture, against Middlesex at Lord's, would decide the championship. At that stage in the season, Surrey could not afford to be generous to opponents battling with the vagaries of the Northern line, even though, in the end, Middlesex won the crucial encounter by six wickets and retained the Championship.

103

P. B. H. May, then captain of both Surrey and England was run out by his Glamorgan counterpart, Wilfred Wooller, in the match between the two counties at The Oval on 11 May 1957. The scorebook entry 'run out 10' hides a remarkable incident. May played the ball wide of mid-on and went for the run, but then, thinking he had been caught, carried on towards the pavilion. However, Bernard Hedges, the fielder, missed the catch and picked up the ball and threw it to the wicketkeeper. Wooller then took the ball and broke the wicket, May being well out of his ground on the way back to the pavilion. Neither May nor his partner Ken Barrington were on the ball, because if Barrington had run to the other end, there would have been no run out. Equally, if May had watched to see whether or not he had been caught, he might well have made his ground back to the end he started from. Much debate ensued about whether it was sharp practice, but the conclusion seemed to be that the problem only arose because the pavilion was out of the batsman's ground from the Vauxhall end. If May had been batting at the other end, then he would have been in his ground as he walked back to the pavilion, and could not have been run out. The dismissal did Glamorgan no good. Surrey made 259 all out and then took all twenty Glamorgan wickets for 93 runs, Glamorgan scoring 62 in their first innings and exactly half that amount in their second. Wooller made 2 and 1, which was at least better than team-mates Jim McConnon, H. G. Davies, Jim Pressdee and H. D. Davies, who all made 0 and 0.

Other first-class cricketers who have been run out thinking they were caught include A. Tait of Gloucestershire, when playing against Somerset at Taunton in May 1978. The fielder who first of all dropped him at slip and then ran him out was one I. T. Botham. The Rhodesian David Pithey, playing for Oxford University against MCC at Lord's on 10 July 1962, was stumped when he left the crease thinking he had been bowled. Dean Jones, playing for Australia against West Indies in the Second Test at Georgetown, Guyana, on 27 March 1991, was 'bowled' by a no-ball from Courtney Walsh. He heard the rattle of the stumps but not the call of no-ball, and set off to the pavilion, which was beyond extra cover. Carl Hooper, fielding in the slips, rushed in to pick up the ball and uproot a stump to run Jones out. Despite the fact that this dismissal was in direct contradiction of Law 38.2 (which of course everybody knows without it having to be quoted here), Jones was given out, 'run out 3', and

Australia went on to defeat by ten wickets.

Another Australian Jones, Samuel Percy of that ilk, was the last survivor of the 1882 Oval Test which gave birth to the legend of the Ashes, being 89 years old when he died in 1951. In the match itself, his batting life was cut short by a curious piece of fielding by W. G. Grace. The Australian captain, Murdoch, played a ball to leg, and with his partner Jones, ran a single. The Hon. A. Lyttelton, the England wicketkeeper, chased the ball and returned it to the striker's end, where W. G. took it. Jones, having safely made his ground and thinking the ball was now dead, moved out of his ground to pat the pitch down, only to find that Grace then put down the wicket and the square leg umpire gave him out. All in all, Jones' part in the match was less than distinguished. He did not bowl, and batting at No. 10, scored 0 and 6, the second innings being the one cut short by Grace's quick thinking.

During a match between Kent II and Wiltshire II at Trowbridge in 1948, the promising 19-year-old A. E. H. Rutter of Wiltshire was a little luckier. At a fairly early stage of what he felt would be a major innings, he launched himself at a well-flighted leg-break and missed it completely. The wicket was broken by the wicketkeeper, there was a loud appeal, and Rutter made his way back to the pavilion. While he was unbuckling his pads in the changing-room, his captain came in and said that the Kent wicketkeeper, Derek Ufton, had whipped off the bails without the ball in his hands, and anyway, nobody had seen the umpire's finger go up. Rutter was told to return to the crease to see what would happen.

As he was about to step out on to the playing area, midway between the wickets, it occurred to Rutter that the ball might still be in play, so he shuffled furtively along the pavilion railings until he was in line with the popping crease and could not be run out or stumped. He then returned to the crease, and was allowed to carry on batting. The only comment from the umpire was 'Hope you enjoyed your walk.'

Other batsmen have been more final in getting themselves out. Andrew Hilditch was given out 'handled the ball 29' when, as non-striker, he handed the ball back to the bowler. Hilditch was playing for Australia against Pakistan in the Second Test of their series at Perth on 29 March 1979. The bowler, who also appealed, was Sarfraz Nawaz. Australia went on to win by seven wickets, but as the other two batsmen dismissed in Australia's second innings were both run out, no wickets fell to the bowlers. In less serious circumstances, in the summer of 1939, Teddington Town were playing the Surrey Vagrants. F. R. Parker hit the ball straight up, high above his head. Seeing that neither the wicketkeeper nor any fielder was making any attempt to get to the ball, he caught it himself and tossed it back to the bowler. The bowler appealed, and Parker was given out 'handled the ball', probably the most conclusive suicide in cricket history. The bowler said he had appealed for caught and bowled, as that mode of dismissal gives credit to the bowler, but the umpires ruled that the handling happened before the catching, and that was that.

In 1957, in a senior house match at Victoria College, Jersey, a batsman, who remains anonymous, so misjudged a forcing shot off the back foot that he hit his own off stump 33 feet in the direction of extra cover. If you are going to hit your wicket, it is best to do it in style.

In that same year, a fine summer for bizarre dismissals, the match between the Eton Ramblers and the Eton Mission at Eton Manor gave the Ramblers wicketkeeper something to talk about. A snick bounced in and out of his gloves, as they so often do, but this time the ball ricocheted forward and lodged itself firmly between the middle and off stumps, removing the off bail. The wicket-keeper picked the ball out of the woodwork and appealed for the catch. The batsman was given out.

In the Lancashire v. Gloucestershire match at Old Trafford in 1896, the last Lancashire pair were together with the scores level. The Gloucestershire bowler was Fred Roberts, and he put everything into his final ball to batsman Frank Sugg. Sugg went for the winning hit, but was caught. It would have been a tie, except that Roberts had bowled a no-ball, thus giving Lancashire victory by one wicket.

Major A. W. Lupton, then captain of Yorkshire and not a great batsman or bowler, was given out stumped by W. B. Franklin off a wide bowled by Jack Newman of Hampshire, in the match between the champions, Yorkshire and MCC at Lord's on 28 August 1925. The same fate befell the great Lancashire and Australia fast bowler, E. A. McDonald, playing for Lancashire against Middlesex at Lord's on 15 June 1929. Mr G. O. 'Gubby' Allen was the bowler, W. F. Price the wicketkeeper. In that innings, the Middlesex and England fast bowler Allen took all ten wickets for 40 runs. As *Wisden* reports that he bowled 'at a fine pace', it is a real curiosity that his ninth victim should have been stumped. In E. W. Swanton's book, *Gubby Allen, Man of Cricket,* he describes the delivery as a 'slow, widish ball'. Later in the season, McDonald was again stumped by Price for the same score, 1, when Lancashire played Middlesex at Old Trafford, but this time the bowler was the less fiery Walter Robins.

To be out hit wicket off a wide is legally possible, but at first-class level has only happened once, to Geoffrey Noblet of South Australia, in their state match against Western Australia at Adelaide on 28 January 1949. He was batting No. 11, with the score at a healthy 419, and his own total 10 when, as *Wisden* reports, 'against the bowling of O'Dwyer, he went after a ball which was called as wide and trod on his wicket. On appeal by O'Dwyer, Noblet was rightly given out "hit wicket" under Laws 29 and 38.' South Australia won the match

easily, and Noblet had his revenge. After taking 4 for 39
in three eight-ball overs, Noblet took over from Gil
Langley as wicketkeeper and stumped O'Dwyer off the
bowling of opening batsman Gogler for 6. This is one of
the few recorded instances of a bowler taking over as a
wicketkeeper and achieving a stumping and a clean
bowled in the same innings.

The often quoted case of a batsman who was clean
bowled and then stumped by the same ball, but still given
not out is probably apochryphal. The story, first noted
in 1892, states that the batsman was given 'not out' by
the umpire at the bowler's end because he did not see the
ball bowled, and 'not out' stumped by the square-leg
umpire, because the batsman had already been bowled.
However, as no appeal is needed for a batsman to be
given out bowled, especially if the square-leg umpire saw
the incident, it seems unlikely that the batsman could
have got away with it.

Possibly the most depressing way to be out is 'run out
0'. Trevor Bailey once wrote an entire chapter in a
cricket coaching manual using that scoreline as his text.
H. Wilson (Northants) has more reason than most to
wince when he sees it in the papers. Wilson made his
debut for the county against the New Zealanders at
Peterborough on 20, 22 and 23 June 1931. Batting at No.
11, in his first innings Wilson was run out for a duck. In
the second innings, coming to the wicket when Northamptonshire needed to add a few more runs to set the
New Zealanders a reasonable target, he had the added

confidence of knowing that his partner at the other end was the opening bat, Fred Bakewell, with over 80 runs to his credit and aiming for his second hundred of the match. *Wisden* records the unhappy result: 'Mr H. Wilson run out 0', while poor Bakewell was left undefeated on 89. Although Wilson excelled himself by taking a wicket, that of Milford 'Curly' Page, the double international at cricket and rugby, in the second innings, Northamptonshire lost by seven wickets, and Wilson never played for his county again. In fact, he never played first-class cricket again, so had only two memories of failing to beat a fielder's return to comfort him in his dotage. He also achieved the curious distinction of playing his entire county career at home, but not in the county he was playing for. Peterborough was not then, and is not now, in Northamptonshire.

A hat-trick of run-outs is unusual. A hat-trick of run-outs to tie a match shows either extreme athleticism on the part of the fielding side or extreme panic by the batsmen. On 1 July 1958, Balliol College, Oxford, played the Marlborough College Common Room at Marlborough. Set to make 127, Balliol had made 119 for 5 with two overs left. Two wickets fell in the penultimate over, the second to a run-out, while four runs were also added, leaving four to win with three wickets in hand as the final over, bowled by Dennis Silk of Cambridge University and Somerset, began. Three runs were scored off the first two balls, and then three men were run out with consecutive balls, two at the bowler's end, one at the striker's end, to tie the match.

Len Hutton was run out for 0 in his first first-class innings, and went on to complete a unique treble – failing to score in his first innings for Yorkshire 2nd XI, for Yorkshire 1st XI and for England. He did get better, though, which the unfortunate Mr Wilson did not.

Marginally less depressing than being run out for 0 is being run out for 99. This has happened to Graham Gooch in a Test match, but also, more disastrously, to 19-year-old John Beck of New Zealand, against South Africa at Cape Town on 2 January 1954. Unlike Gooch, Beck never scored a Test century. Nor did Rusi Surti of India, who was 'c. Burgess b. Bartlett 99' against New Zealand at Auckland on 12 March 1968. He had been dropped twice on 99 before Mark Burgess made certain. As a slight consolation, Surti dismissed Burgess for only 18 as India went on to win the match by 272 runs.

Many cricket games have finished in unusual ways. The Somerset v. Sussex match at Taunton on 21 and 22 May 1920 ended in a remarkable tie. There have been a few first-class games which finished with the scores exactly level like this one (Somerset 243 and 103, Sussex 242 and 104), but no other match in which the final wicket fell by virtue of the last batsman failing to get to the wicket in time. With nine wickets down and the scores level, the final Sussex batsman, Mr H. J. Heygate, who had previously made 0 in the first innings, not bowled and taken no catches, failed to appear promptly. He was crippled with rheumatism at the time, and there had always been some doubt as to whether he would come in to bat. To make sure, one of the Somerset players appealed to umpire Street, who promptly pulled up the stumps and declared the match finished. As *Wisden* remarked, 'Whether or not Heygate would have been able to crawl to the wicket, it was very unsportsmanlike that such a point should have been raised when there remained ample time to finish the match.'

A great finish boiled up in the final of the Mowatt Cup in the early years of this century. The Mowatt Cup, as any educated reader will know, is the Great Northern Railway Inter-Departmental Cricket Cup, and the final was played that year at Cockfosters between the General Manager's Office and Doncaster Locomotive Works. The Doncaster Works XI were batting, the last pair were together and the scores were level, as H. G. Rushton of the General Manager's Office XI ran in to bowl. That the General Manager's Office could field a full eleven implies that overmanning was a real problem on the railways almost a century ago, but H. G. was worth his place in the office for his quick thinking alone. The ball he bowled was not his best, and the Doncaster Works player hit the ball to where mid-off would have been, had H. G. placed a man there. The batsmen set off on what looked like the winning run, but the fleet-footed Rushton dashed for the ball, only to trip as he reached it and tumble in a heap in which ball and bowler became inextricably combined. Finally, Rushton disentangled the ball from his person, and still in a semi-reclining position, he belatedly threw down the wicket at the non-striker's end. The batsman should have been safely home with seconds to spare, but the Great Northern Railway never

had a great reputation for getting there on time. Rushton's electric fielding ensured a tie, because the steam-driven last-wicket pair had stopped in mid-wicket to shake hands and congratulate themselves on the winning run.

Jim Laker's first wicket for Surrey in a county match (his seventh first-class wicket, as he had taken six wickets for the county in a match against the Combined Services earlier in the summer) was against Hampshire at Kingston on 31 August 1946. Laker was bowling to R. N. Exton, that year's captain of the Clifton College side enjoying a summer holiday run in the Hampshire team, batting at No. 8. Laker had Alf Gover fielding at short leg, when Exton launched into one of Laker's few inaccurate balls, straight at the unfortunate Gover. He took immediate evasive action, which involved pulling his sweater up over his head for protection. The ball kept lower than Gover anticipated, however, and hit him between the legs, where it stuck. Mr R. N. Exton, c. Gover b. Laker 7. It sounds routine enough, but none of Laker's other 1,394 wickets for his county came from a catch taken by a fielder with his head deliberately hidden in his sweater.

At Valparaiso Cricket Club in Chile, in 1922, the ball was hit into the pocket of a white tennis cardigan being worn by one of the fielders. Under protest, and probably against the Laws, the batsman was given out.

R. A. Duff, the Australian Test batsman, was unlucky to be run out for 36 in the match between the Australians and Kent at Canterbury on 21 August 1902. He almost played on to a ball from Bradley of Kent, and in doing so left his ground. Huish, the first in a long line of great Kent wicketkeepers, tried to run him out by kicking the ball on to the stumps, but he missed. Duff by this time was attempting a single, but Huish's kick overtook him as he ran to the bowler's end, and the ball hit the far stumps with Duff well out of his ground.

Bishop Charles Wordsworth, of the poetry family, was in the Harrow XI from 1822 to 1825. He later recalled one particularly unfortunate dismissal. 'On one occasion, as I was batting, I knocked the umpire down with a leg hit. Seeing the stroke I was about to make, he turned round; the ball hit him on the back and bounded off into the wicketkeeper's hands. Naturally enough he gave me out, and out I went, under protest. The ball, it is true, had not touched the ground, but if the umpire had not served as twelfth man in the field, it would not have been caught.' A useful lesson in the unfairness of life for a future man of the cloth.

A less useful lesson on the hardness of a cricket ball was taught to a prep school boy in 1957. Fielding rather suicidally at silly-mid-off to the bowling of a slow left armer in a Colts' school match at Aldwickbury, Harpenden, the boy survived several near misses in the course of the first four balls of the over. On the fifth ball, a wicket fell. The new batsman was left-handed, but silly-mid-off, and quite possibly the bowler, failed to notice. Silly-mid-off thus became silly-mid-on, without any question the most dangerous place on the field for an eleven-year-old to be. With the final ball of the over, the new batsman launched into a lofted on drive off a rank half volley. The ball smacked into the central point of silly-mid-on's forehead, and bounced straight back to the wicketkeeper, who caught it. Two players then left the field, the batsman cursing his luck and the fielder, carried unconscious to the san. It is believed he was revived with copious draughts of Ministry of Food orange juice, but ever thereafter fielded a long way away from the bat.

115

Martin Young, Gloucestershire's opening batsman, was 'c. Sharpe b. Illingworth 12' in the match against Yorkshire at Bristol on 25 July 1962. The scoreline does not tell the full story. He hit the ball very hard to short leg,

where Brian Close was fielding. The ball hit Close on the temple, and bounced in a gentle arc to Phil Sharpe at first slip. Close shook himself and carried on as though nothing had happened. When a concerned team-mate asked Close, 'What would have happened if he hit you between the eyes?', Close replied, 'He'd have been caught at cover.'

A hat-trick by a fielder is a rare event. Mark Lockett of Charfield achieved the feat in 1978, Dave Bennett being the lucky bowler. Jack Fakley of Saltwood, standing at gully, also took three catches with consecutive balls, in 1967. A hat-trick of stumpings has only happened once in first-class cricket, when W. H. Brain of Gloucestershire made three consecutive stumpings off the bowling of C. L. Townsend, against Somerset at Cheltenham in 1893. George Dawkes of Derbyshire, in 1958, and Jack Russell of Gloucestershire and England are the only other wicketkeepers to manage a hat-trick in first-class cricket, in each case by means of three catches. Russell took three catches in three balls for Gloucestershire against Surrey at The Oval in 1986, but they were not all off the same bowler. The first was off the sixth ball of Courtney Walsh's over, and the next two came from the first two balls of Syd Lawrence's over from the other end.

Playing for Ealing against Charlton Park on 15 June 1922, A. D. Morton took six catches, all off the bowling of G. Tautz. Tautz took 8 for 28 altogether, including four wickets in four balls, but not including a hat-trick of catches by Morton. K. Webb, playing for the Whitbread Sports and Social Club against Southgate County Old Boys at Woodford Green on 11 August 1963, caught each of the first six Old Boys at first slip. The record for catches in a first-class innings by anybody other than a wicketkeeper remains seven, first performed by Micky Stewart of Surrey against Northamptonshire at Northampton in 1957, and matched by Tony Brown of Gloucestershire against Nottinghamshire at Trent Bridge in 1966. Walter Hammond, perhaps the greatest slip fielder ever, took ten catches in a match for Gloucestershire against Surrey at Cheltenham in 1928, and also scored a century in each innings, 139 in the first and 143 in the second. (By coincidence, the only other time that a player called Hammond had taken as many as six catches in an innings was in August 1793, and the victims were again Surrey.) In the very next match, on 18 August, against Worcestershire, Walter Hammond took nine wickets for 23 runs in the first innings and caught the tenth man off the bowling of Charlie Parker. Before the day was out, he had top-scored for Gloucestershire with 80, making it quite a profitable couple of days' work.

Some cricket teams spread their efforts more evenly. When Middlesex played Essex at Lord's on 8, 10 and 11 June 1963, they won by 158 runs, in no small part due to the all-round fielding performance. Every member of the Middlesex team took at least one catch, the last man falling to Don Bennett's second of the match. Furthermore, nobody took a catch in both innings. In the first Essex innings, catches were taken by Drybrough, Gale (2), wicketkeeper Murray (2) and Parfitt. In the second innings, the catchers were Bennett (2), Bick (caught and bowled), Hooker, Moss (caught and bowled), Price, Russell and White.

At the other end of the scale, J. W. Dale of Cambridge University apologized to his captain Walter Yardley for dropping a catch during the Varsity match of 1870 with the words 'Sorry, Walter, I was looking at a lady getting out of a drag.' All the same, Cambridge managed to scrape home by 2 runs, thanks to F. C. Cobden's famous hat-trick at the very end.

118

OVERTHROWS

All ten wickets for a wicketkeeper
Donald Newton (5 stumped, 3 caught, 2 run out) in Ireland, 1960s

Given out 'Stood Foul'
Wisbech v. Hertfordshire Militia, 1801

Given out 'Absent without Leave 0'
J. Berry, Bradford and Dalton v. Sheffield, 1847

Given out 'Shambled out 1'
T. Cruttenden, Mayfield and Eastern Division v. Wadhurst, at Wadhurst, Jul 1796

Hat-trick of stumpings
Len Hopwood, Cheshire v. Staffordshire, 1926
K. C. James, off W. E. Merritt, for the New Zealanders in Ceylon, 10 Oct 1927
K. V. Bhandarkar, Holkar CA v. Ceylon CA, 1948
Howard Wilmot, off C. Fawcett, Marden Bridge U-13 v. King's Tynemouth U-13, Jun 1980

'Hit-wicket' really meaning headwear falling on stumps
C. G. Taylor, hit wkt b. Hillyer 89, Gentlemen v. Players, 1843
D. Kenyon, hit wkt b. Jepson 64, Worcestershire v. Nottinghamshire, 1949
J. Solomon, hit wkt b. Benaud 4, West Indies v. Australia, 1961

D. Vengsarkar, hit wkt b. Thomson 48, India v Australia, 1977
A. Mankad, hit wkt b. Old 43, India v. England, 1974
D. C. S. Compton, hit wkt b. Miller 184, England v. Australia, 1948

Non-striker run out going for fourth run on first ball of match
Ken Lewsey, Saltwood v. Evington at Evington, 1971

Run-out by fielder kicking ball on to stumps
V. M. Merchant (India) by D. C. S. Compton (Arsenal, Middx & England), The Oval, 1946

Throwing a cricket ball 100 yards while standing in a tub
Henry 'Tabs' Taberer (South Africa), 1902

119

Stumped off a wide
C. Z. Harris (New Zealand), st. Moin Khan b. Iqbal Sikander 13, in World Cup semi-final v. Pakistan, Auckland, 21 Mar 1992

ILLEGAL ACTIONS

10

Cricket is the only major sport ruled by Laws rather than Rules, so it is perhaps not surprising that cricket has come into conflict with the law from time to time. As early as 1853, the match between Lynn and Litcham at King's Lynn produced a legal battle. The match took place on 9 June that year, and during the course of the afternoon, the Lynn captain, whose name was Bagge, needed to call upon his substitute fielder, a man called Holmes. Almost immediately, Bagge took exception to his new fielder's conduct on the field, and an argument developed between captain and twelfth man, who clearly had lunched not wisely but too well. Bagge

then ordered Holmes to leave the field, but Holmes refused, and was therefore forcibly removed. Holmes subsequently brought an action for assault (Holmes v Bagge and another), as a result of which he was awarded £20 damages. The judge, clearly not a cricketer, ruled that the inebriate Holmes had an equal right to occupy any part of the ground as any other member of the club. If a drunken MCC member attempted to stand at second slip during a Test match at Lord's one hundred and forty years on, it seems unlikely that the precedent of Holmes v. Bagge and another would be a workable defence in any action that might arise.

Fights break out on cricket pitches from time to time. Dennis Lillee squared up to Javed Miandad in a Test match in Australia in 1981, and George Muirhead of Heckmondwike was banned for the rest of the season for striking out at two opponents, Clive Jackson and Tommy Mason of Altofts, when he was given out lbw in 1980. Bowlers have shoulder-charged batsmen (e.g. John Snow against Sunil Gavaskar, Lord's 1971) and umpires (e.g. Colin Croft against umpire Goodall at Christchurch in 1980), and bowlers and batsmen have used stumps and

bats to make their opinions better understood (e.g. Raman Lamba and Rashid Patel in the final of the Duleep Trophy in 1991). Only one man, however, has tried to strangle his fiancée at Lord's with his MCC tie, an event which occurred after the 1989 NatWest Final. The man was given a two-year suspended sentence at the Old Bailey the following February, and presumably needed both a new fiancée and a new tie.

122

Other cricket equipment besides the MCC mustard and tomato tie has been used for illegal purposes. In 1975, Mrs Doreen Driscoll (40), a nurse at Hortham Hospital, Almondsbury, was fined £75 for striking a mental patient across the buttocks with a cricket bat. Sri Lankan drug squad detectives became suspicious when they found six cricket balls in the luggage of a German tourist in 1986. They sliced open the balls, and found them to be full of hashish. The German was arrested and – presumably – charged under Law 42, subsection 5, ('Changing the Condition of the Ball').

The most regular link between cricket and the law is when streakers appear. Cricket being a summer game, there are occasionally days, even in England, when the urge to take off all your clothes seems irresistible, and the first case at a first-class game seems to have been on the Saturday of the 1975 Lord's Test between England and Australia, when a man called Michael Angelow ran from the Grandstand seats across the pitch, hurdled the stumps and ran towards the Mound Stand, where he was detained by the police. He was subsequently fined £20 for disorderly conduct. Three females at the WACA ground

n Perth became the first ladies to streak at a first-class match, during the match between Western Australia and South Australia. They too were charged with disorderly conduct. Two streakers appeared at a charity match at Hartley Wintney, Hampshire, in February 1988, but it was so cold that they had done two laps of the ground before the crowd were able to sex them (they were male). The BBC tape of the naked lady who performed a cartwheel in front of the pavilion at Lord's during the 1990 Test series has never been broadcast, but it is a much admired piece of camera work within the Corporation.

Cricket is, quite astonishingly, seen by some people as a nuisance. In 1977, Mr and Mrs J. Miller were awarded £174 against Lintz CC in respect of 'damage and nuisance caused by sixes hit into their property'. Mr Dennis Lovesey of Holton-Le-Clay drove his truck on to the middle of the pitch during the match against Barton-on-Humber in

1985, and refused to move it until spectators at the match removed their cars from the approach lane to his house. Play was held up for half an hour while the cars were moved.

Mr Lovesey's action was unofficial, but that of the police in Port-of-Spain, Trinidad, in 1991 was entirely official. They stopped a match on Queens Park Savannah by issuing parking tickets to players and umpires who had parked their cars by the side of the ground. All those with cars had to move them to an approved parking place before the match could continue.

Another official action was the strike called by Derby Corporation busmen in 1976, in support of their colleagues dismissed for playing cricket during working hours. They were clearly not willing to accept the decision as it stood, and 'all out' took on new meaning for the cricketing busmen.

Militant busmen are not as disconcerting as militant students, though. Aftab Gul, who played for Lahore and Pakistan, and toured England in 1971, was a law student at the Punjab University. In the winter of 1968–69, he became the first man to play first-class cricket while on bail for alleged political activities, and it was said that he owed his selection for the Lahore Test against England in February 1969 to the fact that the authorities did not dare play a Test there without him in the side. He opened the batting and made 12 and 29, but the match was nevertheless often interrupted by what were described as 'minor riots and skirmishes'. The match finished in a draw, and Aftab Gul was dropped for the next match at

Dacca (now Bangladesh) a week later. In 1983, Aftab
applied for political asylum in Britain after two ground-
to-air missiles were seized at his home in Lahore. He
remains the only Test cricketer to be charged with storing
weapons of mass destruction in his garage.

Crime does not stop merely because a cricket match is
in progress. One of literature's greatest thieves, Raffles,
was also a great cricketer, and many real-life pavilions
have been burgled during a match. PC Brian Arkle suddenly ran from the field during his innings for Gateshead
Fell in their match against Durham City in 1991, having
spotted an intruder in the pavilion. He arrested the man,
and then returned to complete his maiden century and
lead his side to victory.

Kevin Lyons was not so fortunate while umpiring the
Leicestershire v. Nottinghamshire match at Leicester at
the very end of August 1988. His car, which contained
all his umpiring clothes, was stolen overnight so he had
to officiate the next day in pinstriped trousers, setting a
standard of sartorial elegance on the cricket field that had
not been seen since Ranji's silk turbans.

The Grasshoppers had mixed success in a match against unnamed opponents in London in July 1939. The match was due to start at 11.30, but began 'only after a great deal of persuasion on the part of the Grasshoppers' at about 1 p.m. The home team was dismissed in next to no time for 15, and they then insisted that the Grasshoppers face one over before lunch. In that one over they scored the 16 runs necessary to win, but despite the easy victory, 'a further experience awaited them. A visitor to their dressing-room took all the valuables and money he could lay hold of.' We get the impression from the report that the fixture would not have been repeated in 1940, even if Hitler had not invaded Poland.

John Shilton, a slow-left-arm bowler who played for Warwickshire at the end of the nineteenth century, was never lucky in his dealings with bookmakers or the law. A few days before his benefit match, awarded in 1895, he was arrested for debt and taken into custody. The club paid his debts in order to allow him to play, but there was no happy ending. He died just a few years later, in 1899, at the age of about 42. His obituary in *Wisden* notes that 'Shilton was personally quite a character, but

though he had his faults, this is not the place in which to dwell upon them.'

Edward Pooley, the Surrey wicketkeeper, missed out on a Test cap by being stuck in a New Zealand jail while his team-mates were playing the first ever Test match in Melbourne. Touring Australia and New Zealand as first choice wicketkeeper with James Lillywhite's team in the winter of 1876–77, Pooley found ways of augmenting his income in the same way as later wicketkeepers such as Godfrey Evans and Rod Marsh; he liked to strike a few bets. In Christchurch, he bet a local man, Ralph Donkin, £1 to a shilling that he could forecast the scores of each member of the Eighteen of Canterbury that they were due to play the next day. Donkin fell for the trick, and Pooley bet that each man would score nought. After the game, Pooley then claimed £1 for each duck, and offered to pay one shilling for each player (actually, fewer than half the side) who got off the mark. By the terms of the bet, Donkin owed Pooley around £10. However, as might be expected, a fight ensued, and Pooley was charged with assault and malicious damage. Although he was eventually acquitted of the charges, he missed the boat to Australia and with it his only chance of Test cricket.

An equally final exit from the international field of play was achieved in Turkey at the turn of the century. An unnamed Turkish naval officer, playing cricket with the Europeans at the Candilli Club in Constantinople in 1901, aroused the suspicions of the authorities and was arrested as a spy by the Turkish cavalry. He refused to surrender until he had finished his innings, however, so the cavalry

127

stood by until he was bowled, and then carried him off. No word of what happened to him was ever received. As the reporter of this event remarked, 'One feels that he deserved a better fate.'

Less of a crime but equally concerned with the law is the blissful state of marriage. Cricket and marriage do not mix, and at least one fanatical club cricketer has been divorced by his wife because of his unreasonable devotion to the game. He was reported to be away on a cricket tour at the time and therefore unable to comment to the press on the action.

The Duke of Hamilton met his future bride, Miss Burrell, at a grand cricket match at Sevenoaks in June 1777, 'where his Grace was observed to pay an uncommon degree of attention to this lady during the whole entertainment'. The match was between England and Hambledon, in which James Aylward, the great left-handed batsman, scored 167 spread over two days, but we may safely assume that the Duke and Miss Burrell did not pay him too much attention.

Two centuries later, however, bride stopped play. In 1987, the match between Charter Sports and Morehall, at Ashford, was held up at the request of a couple who were holding their wedding reception in the pavilion at the time. The bride wanted some of her wedding photos taken out on the pitch, so play was stopped while the bride posed at the wicket, bat and bouquet in hand, with her groom in the slips.

From there it is only a short step to the captain's wife fielding as substitute, something that happened at Yoxford

in Suffolk in 1976, when the local side was a man short but the teas were already under control. And nature being what it is, one of the occupational hazards of marriage is childbirth, especially childbirth during the cricket season. In 1990, Andrew Matthewan was batting for Green Moor against Carlton Community Club in the Barnsley League when his wife Beverley went into labour. Still wearing his whites (though having discarded pads, gloves and helmet), Andrew rushed his wife to the local hospital, where she soon gave birth to a healthy daughter. He then returned to the match, to find his own innings over, but with still enough time to run the final Carlton batsman out to give his side victory.

However, human nature being what it is, not all love stories end happily. Jamaican fast bowler Leslie Hylton, who played six Tests in the 1930s, was executed in 1955 for the murder of his wife.

CURIOUS
MATCHES AND
MOMENTS

11

One of the complaints that is most often expressed about the best loved game by those who do not best love it is that it seems to go on for ever. Indeed, for many years, Test matches were deemed to be 'timeless', played to a finish, however long that might take. In fact, the longest such Test was only ten days long, ending on 14 March 1939, with the match still undecided. It was the final Test, and the final game, of the MCC tour to South Africa, and the match was left unfinished at the end of the tenth playing day, with England needing 42 runs to win, with five wickets in hand. The problem was that the match was being played in Durban, and the MCC tourists had to catch their ship back to England from Cape Town, a two-day train ride away.

If ten days seems like a long time for a cricket match to last, spare a thought for 18 teenagers of Belper, in Derbyshire, who in 1983 claimed a world record by playing non-stop for 316 hours, which is 13 days and four hours. The result, if any, is not known.

The longest match of all was probably the game between teams led by the Earl of Winchelsea and Mr R. Leigh, which began on Stoke Down in Hampshire on 23

July 1795. Three days were set aside for the match, but by the end of 25 July, Mr R. Leigh's XI still needed 36 runs to win, with seven wickets standing. Eventually, the two elevens reassembled on 28 June of the following year, when the runs were obtained for the loss of four more wickets, giving Mr R. Leigh's team victory by three wickets, 339 days after the first ball was bowled.

Some matches which ought to have finished quickly actually lasted a little longer than expected. When Willie Oates turned up to play for Wentworth against Rotherham on Thursday 10 June 1880, he discovered he was the only member of his side to have turned up. There had been a tremendous thunderstorm in the morning, and all the rest of his side had assumed the pitch would be flooded and the match abandoned. However, all the Rotherham players made it, in spite of the weather, and the spectators were obviously keen to see a game of cricket. So Mr Oates, who incidentally was a resident of Rotherham and was only playing for Wentworth for old times' sake as the place where he spent his youth, recruited ten bystanders to make up a side, and then won the toss. He opened the batting, scored 43 of his side's total of 93 (which says quite a lot for the other ten press-ganged to Wentworth's cause) and then opened the bowling. When not bowling, he kept wicket, and ended up with seven wickets and a stumping, as Rotherham, collapsed to 72 all out and defeat by 21 runs. The last man was caught by one W. Trueman off Oates with two minutes to play.

Eight years later, E. M. Grace, W. G.'s coroner brother, virtually duplicated Oates' feat, when playing for

Thornbury against Dursley at Dursley in July 1888. Only three Thornbury men turned up, E. M., C. J. Robinson and F. L. Cole. Nothing daunted, Dr Grace recruited eight rustics, and like Oates before him, won the toss. He and Robinson put on 147 for the first wicket, but then disaster – Cole and the other eight made only nine runs between them. However, Grace then bowled Dursley out twice, taking 14 wickets in the process, and Thornbury won by an innings.

Darlington CC beat Synthonia CC in June 1990 without a run coming off the bat, thanks to a travel mix-up which resulted in only two members of the Synthonia side turning up for the match. Synthonia batted first (what else could they do?), but Steven Eland, fifty per cent of the Synthonia side, was bowled fourth ball for a duck, leaving the other fifty per cent not out for 0. The Synthonian pair then persuaded nine of the Darlington players to act as substitutes while Eland bowled the opening over. The fourth ball, sadly, was a wide, so Darlington had won, without willow ever being put on ball in anger (except possibly by the Synthonian duo after the match, in frustration at their colleagues' non-arrival). The same feat was achieved by Cawood in the York Senior League in 1979. They dismissed rivals Dringhouses, fielding a full eleven men, for just two, and the winning runs then came as four byes off the first ball of the Cawood innings.

In 1977, Rupert Murdoch's Australian newspaper, the *Sun*, ran a 'Computer Test' between England and Australia to coincide with the Centenary Test being played in Melbourne that March. Neither weather nor time had any real effect on the match, which Australia won by three wickets. In England's first innings of 360, W. G. Grace made 86, Jack Hobbs 62 and Harold Larwood a vigorous 51 towards the end of the innings, and they went on to gain a first innings lead of 15, despite Victor Trumper's brilliant 109, the only century of the match. England's second innings was a disaster, despite Jack Hobbs making another big score, 76. Dennis Lillee, the only man playing in both the real and the computerized Centenary Test, took 6 for 80 as England tumbled to 225 all out. Needing 241 to win, Australia got there with three wickets in hand, thanks largely to Neil Harvey's patient 64. The result of the real Centenary Test was much more of a curiosity. It ended in a win for Australia by 45 runs, exactly the same margin as in the first ever Test match a hundred years before.

OVERTHROWS

Blues v. Heartaches
at Peper Harrow, 21 Jun 1981

Final played between beaten semi-finalists because winners refused to meet
Central Electricity Generating Board (North-West Region) Cup Final
Pennine TD (Preston) beat Padiham PS (Burnley) by 19 runs, 26 Aug 1988

Frothblowers v. Non-Frothblowers
Kobe, Japan, 1927

Ladies v. Gentlemen
at Houghton Regis, 1949

Maids of Hambledon v. Maids of Bramley
19 Jun 1977

One Arm v. One Leg
13 Jul 1863
Stoolball match at Lord's
W.W. Grantham KC's XI v. the Japanese Embassy, Sep 1927
Women with Bats v. Men with Hunting Whips
13 Jun 1894
42 consecutive county matches without a draw
Gloucestershire, 27 Jul 1920 to 4 Jul 1922

Some things that happen in the pursuit of a game of cricket are indefinable, but still curious. How do you classify a tug-of-war to decide for which side in a Test match one of the players turns out? In February 1896, some sources say a tug-of-war was held to decide whether Major R. M. Poore should play for England or South Africa in the series that was about to begin. The South Africans won, and Poore played for them, although it was said he would have preferred to play for England.

Where do you file the odd fact that between 25 March 1947 and 10 July 1975, no cricketer sporting a moustache played for England? The England career of Peter Smith, the Essex spinner, ended in two days of torrential rain at Lancaster Park, Christchurch, New Zealand, and it was

not until 28 years and 107 days later that another hairy gent from Essex, one G. A. Gooch, made his Test debut in the First Test against Australia at Edgbaston and reintroduced moustaches to the England dressing-room. Gooch scored fewer runs in the two innings of his debut (0) than Smith did in the one innings of his final Test (1). There was a gap of 28 years and 122 days between the scoring of runs by men with moustaches for England, as Gooch finally got off the mark on 31 July 1975 in the Second Test at Lord's. It was not long before people from other parts of the country took the fashion lead of Essex. Geoff Miller and Ian Botham both sported moustaches halfway between their England caps and England sweaters before the decade was out, and in the Eighties, upper lip hair became the norm rather than the exception for England cricketers.

Under which heading do you put the reference to cricket in 'Don Quixote' by Cervantes, written in about 1600? And this reference is not of the Biblical tennis reference type: 'And Joseph served in the courts of Pharaoh.' In the English translation of Chapter 19 of the Second Part of Cervantes' masterpiece, Basilius is described as 'the most active youth we know: a great pitcher at the bar, an excellent wrestler, a great player at cricket, runs like a buck, leaps like a wild goat, and plays ninepins as if by witchcraft.' This caused great excitement in the correspondence columns of *The Cricketer*, as references to cricket anywhere in the world were rare in the sixteenth century, let alone in Spain. Unfortunately, the reference turns out to be the invention of English translator Charles

Jarvis. The original describes Basilius as a '*gran jugador de pelota*', which is a very different game from cricket.

There is at least one work in Spanish on cricket. *La Tranca* (The Wicket) was published almost three hundred years after *Don Quixote* hit the bookstalls of Madrid, in Buenos Aires in February 1881. It included a glossary of cricketing terms translated into Spanish, including the rather obscure *bola-punzadora*, meaning 'a shooter', and the more obvious *el batador* and *el boleador*.

The connection between cricket and literature is consistently strong over the years, with many great artists and writers, from Sir Arthur Conan Doyle to Harold Pinter being avid followers of cricket. Trevor Howard used to have a clause in his movie contracts stating that he would not be required for filming, during a Lord's Test, and in 1962 moved the matinee of his London stage hit from the Thursday to the Wednesday for one week in June so as not to miss the first day's play of the Second Test against Pakistan. Sir C. Aubrey Smith is the only England Test captain to receive a knighthood in acknowledgement of his Hollywood career.

Trevor Howard took part in one of the more statistically satisfying events of minor cricket, when he played for Brian Johnston's team against the village of Widford in Hertfordshire on 24 June 1962. The match was a 12-a-side game, and each of Johnston's eleven bowlers took one wicket. Johnners himself was the twelfth man, the wicketkeeper, who did not take a wicket. His team included not only Trevor Howard, but also journalists Michael Melford, John Woodcock and Robin Marlar (who needed three overs to take his wicket, whereas the Pakistan touring team's assistant manager, Major Rahman, obliged in his first over), Sir Pelham Warner's son John, as well as Test cricketers such as Russell Endean and J. P. Fellows-Smith.

Samuel Beckett is the only Nobel prize winner to have played first-class cricket. His obituary in the 1990 *Wisden* points out that he played two first-class games for Dublin University against Northamptonshire in 1925 and 1926. He was a left-handed batsman and a left-arm medium pace bowler. On 18 and 20 July 1925, batting at No. 8, he scored 18 and 12, and was hit for 17 runs in his eight overs, without taking a wicket. The University lost by an innings and 56 runs. On 7 and 8 July 1926, he was less successful, although he had been promoted to opening batsman. He scored just 4 and 1, making him one of the select band of first-class cricketers who have top scored in their first innings, and then seen their run tally decline in each innings thereafter throughout their entire career. In 1926, he took 0 for 47 in 15 overs, but did take two catches as the University slumped to defeat by an innings and 241 runs. He was dismissed twice in the two matches by one E. F. Towell, and in his final innings he was dismissed by the first ball that S. C. Adams ever bowled in first-class cricket.

H. G. Wells inherited his love of cricket from his father, Joseph Wells, who was a fast round-arm bowler, but not much of a batsman. On 26 June 1862, playing for Kent against Sussex at the Royal Brunswick Ground at Hove, Wells took six wickets for 35 runs, all bowled, including

four wickets in four balls, the only time this feat was achieved in major cricket by a round-arm bowler. His victims were, in order of disappearance, one James Dean, Spencer Austen-Leigh, C. H. Ellis and Richard Fillery. The literary connections of Wells's achievement are truly magnificent, because his second victim, Spencer Austen-Leigh, was one of seven brothers, all great-nephews of Jane Austen. Between the seven of them, they played for Eton, Harrow, Cheltenham, Cambridge University, Oxford University, Sussex, Gloucestershire, Berkshire and the Gentlemen of Kent.

In 1900, P. G. Wodehouse played for Dulwich College's First XI, and in the same year A. A. Milne was playing for Westminster School. Lord Byron played for Harrow against Eton in 1805, and 101 years later Rupert Brooke was chosen for Rugby against Marlborough at Lord's. John Keats recorded in a letter dated 19 March 1819 that 'yesterday I got a black eye whilst taking up a cricket bat. Brown, a friend in disaster, applied a leech to my eyelid and there is no inflammation this morning. I am glad it was not a clout.'

Those poets of the modern age, the rock musicians,

have treated cricket generously. Roy Harper's 1975 classic 'When An Old Cricketer Leaves The Crease' was one of the first rock songs to be built around cricket, and 10 cc (standing for 'cubic centimetres', not 'cricket club') hit number one in the UK singles charts in September 1978 with 'Dreadlock Holiday', which included the immortal line, 'I don't like cricket, I love it.' In more recent years, Rory Bremner, under the pseudonym of The Commentators, took his song based around David Gower's 1984 Test batting average, 'N-N-N Nineteen Not Out' to number 13 in the charts during the summer of 1985 (when Gower did rather better in the Tests). In 1984 in Australia, an anonymous Richie Benaud imitator, calling himself The Twelfth Man, took his unbroadcastable but very funny 'It's Just Not Cricket' to number one. The victorious 1970–71 MCC team that toured Australia recorded 'The Ashes Song' on their return, but fortunately for humanity, it was not a hit.

Other cricketers have made records. Don Bradman made a record (Columbia DB270) in 1930, called 'How It's Done', but either he didn't explain very well or else nobody listened to it, because even after it was released, he was still the only person who could bat that brilliantly. 'Our Don Bradman' by Art Leonard, recorded in 1934, was a light vocal tribute to Australia's hero, which is still played from time to time today. Jack Hobbs made three records in the Twenties, including the snappily titled 'How To Improve Your Cricket', and Harold Larwood made 'Leg Theory' (Columbia DB 1140) in 1933. James Cutmore, who scored almost 16,000 runs for Essex in the

1920s and 1930s, is one of the few county cricketers who have made a non-cricketing record. 'Smiling Irish Eyes/Things We Want' (Parlophone R492) featured Cutmore on lead vocals, but as he never made another record, we can assume it did not sell too well. The only county cricketer to be part of a number one hit single is Geoff Hurst, better known as England's hat-trick hero in the World Cup Final at Wembley in 1966, and unfortunately unforgettable as one of many tenors featured on the England World Cup Squad's 1970 number one hit, 'Back Home'. Hurst played once for Essex against Lancashire at Aigburth, Liverpool, from 30 May to 1 June 1962, scoring three less than he did in the World Cup Final in each innings, although he was not out in the first innings.

At least two operettas on the subject of cricket have been written, *Batter Suite, or Not Cricket* by Vivian Ellis, and *Cricket* by Tim Rice and Andrew Lloyd Webber. *Batter Suite* includes the line, 'Granny, when I grow up I'm going to be a soldier and kill the Australians', a sentiment all English cricket followers can understand. The song, 'Sprigs of Nobility We' includes the verse:

140

In every trade and calling take the richest and the
greatest –
Their brains may be appalling, but their bats, you'll
find, were straightest;
While huddle in the jails, or on the gallows dangle
The miserable males whose bats were at an angle,
And those who dropped a sitter or played forward to
half-volleys
In squalor long and bitter must expiate their follies.
(How very true.)

141

Cricket was written to celebrate Her Majesty the
Queen's 60th birthday, and was performed privately at
Windsor Castle. The total audience was no smaller than
for a county match on a cold and misty Thursday morning
at Derby. However, the leading cricket songwriter of the
century is undoubtedly Gerard Durani Martineau, whose
offerings were printed in *The Cricketer* regularly throughout the middle decades of this century. Some of his lyrics
do not stand the test of time, most obviously 'The Gay
Sussex Cricketers', which was published in May 1939.
The chorus ends

Then here's to Sussex cricketers, the braves of bat and
ball,
To the gay Sussex cricketers, the lithe and the tall.
I like the Kentish cricketers
I like the Yorkshire cricketers
I like all kinds of cricketers
But the gay Sussex cricketers
I toast them first of all.

The next week an apology was printed, stating that the word 'lithe' should have been printed as 'little'. Mr Martineau lived in Folkestone, Kent.

A reluctance to play cricket is certainly a curiosity. Two pupils at Brighton College were suspended in the summer term of 1976 for gross disobedience. Their crime was refusing to play for the College against the Old Boys, because they wanted to revise for their 'A' Levels. There is no record either of the result of the match or of their 'A' Levels.

142

Mike Brearley, probably the most academically gifted cricketer since C. B. Fry, batted very low down the order for Cambridge University against Northamptonshire at Fenner's on 6 June 1964. Instead of his usual opening slot, he batted at No. 7, and made a fine 92. The reason for his batting so low in the order was that he had been sitting an examination for entry into the Civil Service. It was later announced that he had come out top in the country in this particular exam.

MEN OF
MANY PARTS

12

Cricketers seem to be the perfect dilettantes, able to turn their hand with complete success to a variety of other pastimes. Several English Test cricketers have also represented their country at football, most recently Willie Watson of Yorkshire and Sunderland, and Arthur Milton of Gloucestershire and Arsenal. Andy Ducat, of Surrey and Arsenal, captained England at football and died playing cricket at Lord's during the Second World War. Denis Compton only played football for England in a wartime international, but his brother Leslie, who kept wicket for Middlesex for many years but never made the England team, did at least win a full England soccer cap. R. E. 'Tip' Foster, scorer of the highest individual score

143

on a Test match debut (287* v. Australia at Sydney in December 1903), is the only man to have captained England at both cricket and football.

C.B. Fry played football and cricket for England, and also held the world long jump record for several years. He was also offered the Kingdom of Albania, but had to refuse because he did not have enough cash to be a successful monarch.

144

Double internationals at cricket and rugby are also comparatively commonplace. M.J.K. Smith played fly-half for England against Wales at Twickenham in 1956, and other double internationals include A.E. Stoddart, A.N. Hornby, R.H. Spooner and G.F. Vernon. S.M.J. 'Sammy' Woods and Frank Mitchell are remarkable treble internationals. Woods played cricket for both England and Australia, and rugby for England, while Mitchell played cricket for both England and South Africa, and rugby for England. He captained South Africa at cricket and England at rugby.

Double internationals at cricket and hockey include the Nawab of Pataudi, who played cricket for both England and India, and hockey for India. Russell Endean played cricket and hockey for South Africa, while Keith Thomson did so for New Zealand and M.J. Gopalan for India. Brian Booth, a captain of Australia at cricket, played hockey for his country at the Melbourne Olympics in 1956, to become one of the few international cricketers also to take part in the Olympic Games. Another crick-eting Olympian was J.W.H.T. Douglas, a boxing gold medal winner at middleweight in London in 1908, and also an amateur soccer international.

Everton Weekes is the only Test cricketer also to be a bridge international, having represented his native Barbados in international bridge tournaments. Percy Sherwell and L.E. 'Doodles' Tapscott both represented South Africa at both cricket and tennis, while Bruce Dooland achieves the most recondite pairing of all, having played for Australia at both cricket and baseball. Sir Richard Hadlee and his wife, Karen, are the only husband and wife to have played for their country at cricket. Terry Alderman and his sister Di Emerson have both represented Australia. Western Australia's captain and Test batsman John Inverarity's daughter Alison reached the final of the high jump at the Barcelona Olympics in 1992.

In 1957–58, the Australian team toured South Africa, and at the end of the tour challenged combined South African teams to two games of baseball. Neil Harvey pitched throughout all nine innings of both games, and Les Favell, as catcher, was another star of the games. Skipper Ian Craig, not a great success with the bat at cricket on that tour, played first base and helped the Australians to victory at baseball to match their success at cricket. Australians also have their own football game, but as they do not seem to play internationals (because no other nation is daft enough to take to the sport), the greatest achievement seems to be that of Vic Richardson, grandfather of the Chappell brothers, who captained his country at cricket and his state (South Australia) at Aussie Rules football. Laurie Nash, who played cricket twice for Australia in the 1930s, but never in the same team as

Richardson, was one of the greatest Aussie Rules players of all time.

These days there is no time to play both cricket and football at the very top level, as the career of Gary Lineker shows. Lineker was good enough as a cricketer in his teens to consider turning professional, but decided on football. He has still found time to become a playing member of MCC, and played for MCC against Germany at Lord's in July 1992, making him a kind of double international. After being out for one, he remarked, 'I always score 1 against Germany'. Andy Goram, the Rangers and Scotland goalkeeper, has also played cricket for Scotland, but was eventually banned by Rangers from playing top-level cricket, for fear of injury.

Chris Balderstone, now a Test umpire, but also a Test cricketer for England, had a long footballing career with Huddersfield Town, Carlisle United and Doncaster Rovers. At the turn of the seasons, his loyalties were divided. On 13 September 1975, he was with his Leicestershire team-mates as they travelled to Chesterfield for their final county match of the season, one which they hoped would confirm them as County Champions. On 14 September, Leicestershire gained a first innings lead of 15, and more importantly earned four bowling points (Balderstone 1 for 13 in nine overs) to win them the title. Then Leicestershire began their second innings. At close of play, Balderstone was 51 not out, and rather than staying to help his colleagues celebrate their Championship, Balderstone set off for Doncaster to don his No. 11 shirt and play in a Fourth Division match against

Brentford. It ended in a 1–1 draw, and Balderstone then set off south again to rejoin his colleagues. The next morning, he took his overnight score to 116 before being run out, thus becoming the only man in history to play a full game of League soccer halfway through a first-class hundred. It is a sobering thought that 6,353 people watched his efforts for Doncaster Rovers in an early season midweek night game in the Fourth Division, probably double the number of people who were there to watch him and his Leicestershire colleagues win the County Championship title for the first time.

Graham Cross is the only man to have played in Cup Finals at both Wembley and Lord's. He gained two runner-up medals for Leicester City in 1963 and 1969, but gained a winner's medal with Leicestershire in the 1975 Benson and Hedges Final. Chris Balderstone was playing in that match, too. Denis and Leslie Compton gained League Championship medals with Arsenal in 1947–48, having been part of the Middlesex Championship-winning side of 1947. Jim Standen, of Worcestershire and West Ham, won an FA Cup winner's medal in May 1964, and went on to earn a Championship medal with Worcestershire later that summer.

THE UMPIRE'S DECISION IS FINAL

13

A cricketer is the personification of sportsmanship. Since the earliest days of stoolball on the Weald of Kent, cricket has been the one sport in which fair play is the only play. Perhaps it is because cricket has Laws while all other games have Rules: people are more likely to bend the Rules than to break the Laws. 'It's not cricket' is the cry wherever the sun never sets, whenever sharp practice is detected. Cricket and absolute integrity walk hand in hand.

This should make the role of the umpire in a cricket match purely ceremonial. This man in a white coat standing magisterially behind the stumps as the bowler bowls, idly tossing stones from hand to hand, and signalling with a series of abstruse arm movements the events as they occur on the pitch, this man draped in sweaters, sunhats and damp towels, this noble gentleman with a spare ball in his pocket is more than just an advanced semaphore practitioner, more than just a living coat rack. He is the embodiment of calm authority in a gentle game, a well-loved figurehead to all those at whose games he officiates. He is a pillar of perfection in an imperfect world. He is the umpire.

It seems odd, therefore, that the umpires take part in   149
so many of the curiosities that dot cricket literature.
'Umpire ducked in pond for giving unsatisfactory decision'
was a statement recorded after the Benenden v. Penshurst
game of 1892, and even such a pillar of probity as Lord
Cobham wrote, after a House Cup match at Eton at the
end of the last century: 'Both Mitchell and I were supposed
to have been "chisselled" [sic] out by the umpires, and
both of them were "ducked" accordingly. Old Joby was
one, Picky Powell probably the other. The ducking did
not come to much.' The callousness of the word 'probably'
is what stands out. At Eton, they obviously ducked
umpires regularly, regardless of whether they got the right
man or not.

Old Joby and Picky Powell should be pleased that they
were umpiring at Eton College, and not in Pakistan. In
1977, it was reported that 'three students at Karachi
College have been charged with killing an umpire during
a friendly school match, after he refused to reverse a
decision.' I am unable to find out what sentence was
passed on the three cricketers, but it must have been hard
to find volunteers to umpire in serious matches at Karachi

College, if death was the solution to doubtful decisions in friendly games.

More recently, in June 1992, one Bryn Derbyshire, 37, of Thoresby Road, Bramcote, was given a three-month suspended sentence at Nottingham Crown Court and ordered to pay £400 compensation to Mr Joseph Purser, after being found guilty of 'causing bodily harm by wanton furious driving'. In a cricket context, 'wanton furious driving' conjures up images of Ian Botham or 'Croucher' Jessop in their batting prime, but their aggressive batsmanship never landed them in the dock. Mr Derbyshire had been given out lbw by Mr Purser in a match between Old Park, Nottingham, and Blyth, and after the match reversed his car at the umpire, who injured himself jumping out of the way. As all club cricketers will acknowledge, no batsman has ever been out lbw, whatever the bowler, the wicketkeeper, three slips, gully, square leg and the umpire may think, but Mr Derbyshire's answer to a doubtful decision is not generally to be recommended.

Umpires in village cricket, as Charles Ponsonby remarked in a letter to *The Times* in 1935, 'are all honourable men and try to temper their judgements with discretion, but the majority have no training in the art of umpiring, and many would frankly admit that they are unfit for cricket, too old, too fat or too slow. Some even have defective dental arrangements which interfere with a quick decision. I was playing in a match last year and as the bowler delivered the ball, the umpire ejaculated "brrr", and after a pause, "I beg your pardon, I meant

to say no-ball, but I dropped my teeth".'

That umpires have always been upholders of the law is evidenced from a report in *The Times* of 10 October 1787: 'Two Justices of the Peace sent their mandate to stop a game at cricket; but the messenger was desired to return with the players' humble service, and if they might depend on justice being done them, they would be glad if the worthy Magistrates, for the sake of the peace, would do them the honour of coming to be umpires.'

Umpires have, of course, from time to time given incorrect decisions. The statement, 'I didn't see it, but I give him out' was first recorded at a Royston v. Littleborough game in 1891. In a schoolboys' game at Tenterden Hall, Hendon, on Whit Monday 1922, the umpires on four occasions gave seven balls to the over. This is not in itself a rare occurrence, although it says little for the umpires' mathematical skills, but as *The Cricketer* records, 'on each occasion a boy was out. One boy suffered thus in both innings'. That boy will no doubt have wished he was old enough to drive a car at the umpire in a wanton furious manner. It is not recorded whether he was given out lbw on either occasion.

In July 1848, according to a report in the *Guardian*, the match between Knutsford Royal Albert and Congleton had to be abandoned because of disputes over 'the correctness of the decision of the Congleton umpire' after Mr Drinkwater of Knutsford had been given out caught. The Knutsford players refused to continue the match unless the Congleton umpire was replaced. The Secretary of the Knutsford club, in a letter to the newspaper a few days later, stated that 'the reason was not solely on account of the decision then given, but also of *three* previous ones, which, not to impute the motive of unfairness, showed at least such inattention or want of knowledge of the game, that the Knutsford players decided that they could have no pleasure in continuing the game.'

Cricket has no tradition of sending players off for bad behaviour, although it may not be long before this becomes the norm. Only three players in first-class cricket in England have been sent off, and then each time by their captain. The Hon. Lionel Tennyson, captain of Hampshire, dismissed J. A. Newman, his main bowler, during his county's game against Nottinghamshire at

152

Trent Bridge. Newman had refused to bowl because the crowd were barracking him, so his captain ordered him from the field. As he left, Newman kicked down the stumps, which *Wisden* described as 'a most unusual display of petulance from a likeable man'. The second captain to reduce his own numbers by one was another nobleman, Lord Hawke of Yorkshire, who finished the career of the great left-arm spinner Bobby Peel by ordering him off the field during Yorkshire's game with Middlesex at Sheffield in 1897, and never allowing him to be picked for the county again. Peel's sin was to come on to the field under the influence of alcohol. One version states that 'Peel fell down after entering the playing area and was helped up by Lord Hawke' but a more widely held if unsubstantiated version is that Peel relieved himself against the boundary fence in full view of the crowd. The commoner Brian Bolus, captaining Derbyshire against his former county Yorkshire at Chesterfield on 18 June 1973, sent his opening bowler Alan Ward home before the close of play, for refusing to bowl. Two days later Ward announced his retirement.

Dr W. G. Grace was famous for disputing umpires' decisions. When Joe Filliston gave him out lbw in a London County game at Crystal Palace, W. G. refused to leave the crease. As nobody had the courage to contradict him, he continued his innings. In minor matches, Grace often simply refused to be out, on the grounds that 'these people have come to see me bat, not to see you bowl'.

These days disputes with the umpires are no longer curiosities. Mike Gatting's notorious dispute with the

Pakistan umpire Shakoor Rana cost one day's play in the Second Test at Faisalabad in December 1987. The third day's play, on 9 December, was entirely lost as a result of a decision by Shakoor Rana, at square leg, to stop play as Hemmings ran up to bowl because he felt that Mike Gatting, as England's captain, had been unfairly moving David Capel at deep square leg without informing the batsman Salim Malik. As *Wisden* tells the story, 'Gatting informed the umpire that he was, in his opinion, over-stepping his bounds. The language employed throughout the discourse was basic'. A full day was lost as Shakoor Rana refused to take any further part until Gatting had apologized, and England's potentially winning position was allowed to slip. With the final twenty overs about to begin, Pakistan were 51 for 1, chasing a target of 239 to win. 'In keeping with the conduct of everything to do with the match,' writes *Wisden*, 'Miandad called his batsmen in when the last twenty overs were due to start. That the Laws make no provision for such an early closure did not prevent the umpires from drawing stumps immediately.' The match was not awarded to England, as by the letter of the Laws, it should have been. In the Third and final Test of the series, the captains agreed to abandon the match at tea on the final day, so this unloved series achieved the doubtful but unique distinction of having the majority of its matches curtailed through lack of interest on the part of the players. The spectators were not very interested either. Fewer than 200 people saw the opening of the series at Lahore on 25 November.

That incident did not develop into a full-scale riot, but

108 years earlier, at the Sydney Cricket Ground, an umpire's decisions did spark off serious civil disobedience. When Lord Harris took a touring side to Australia in 1879, he procured the services of George Coulthard from Melbourne Cricket Club to act as umpire. Unfortunately, although his lordship thought that by using an Australian as umpire he would ensure impartiality and win the support of the crowds, he had not taken into account the natural suspicion of a Melbourne man's efforts in front of a Sydney crowd. Coulthard began to lose public sympathy when, in the match against New South Wales beginning on 7 February 1879, he disallowed an appeal for caught behind against his employer Lord Harris, from a snick that was heard all over the ground. By half-past-three on the Saturday, New South Wales were following on, and Coulthard gave Billy Murdoch, the New South Wales champion batsman, run out when he went for a sharp single with the total on 18. Murdoch made no attempt to disguise his contempt at the decision, and within seconds, spectators had jumped on to the pitch and surrounded poor George Coulthard. For an hour and a half, it was mob rule at SCG, but Lord Harris refused to leave the ground, saying that if his side had done so, New South Wales could have claimed the match. The pitch was finally cleared by five o'clock. The English players refused to countenance a change of umpires, so, under protest, the New South Wales batsmen attempted to restart the match. As soon as the crowd saw that Coulthard was still standing as umpire, they invaded the pitch again. Play was abandoned for the day.

On the Monday, England finished off the New South Welshmen to win by an innings in front of a small and subdued crowd. Coulthard was still umpiring. Lord Harris subsequently blamed the betting element in the crowd for the riot. When Tom Emmett, a Yorkshireman playing for Lord Harris's side, was asked what role he had played in quelling the riot, he replied, 'Nowt. Ah coom to play cricket – not to put down bloody riots.'

156

Crowds have rioted from time to time since then over umpiring decisions. In 1954 at Georgetown, then in British Guiana, crowds threw bottles and police retaliated with tear gas when wicketkeeper Clifford McWatt of West Indies was given run out after a stand of 99 with J. K. Holt, in the Third Test of the series against England. This was the first major crowd disturbance in post-war cricket, but sadly it was not the last. Now they are too commonplace to be described as curiosities. What is curious is that there were no crowd riots during the 1932–33 MCC tour of Australia, so controversially marred by the 'bodyline' tactics of MCC.

Umpires have been faced with many difficult decisions

over the years. Umpire K. McCanlis awarded four leg byes off a ball which struck Somerset captain G. E. S. Woodhouse on the head and bounced off beyond the boundary, in the match between Essex and Somerset at Clacton on 22 August 1949. The bowler was Trevor Bailey. However, when Woodhouse stood up again, it was noticed that the bails were on the ground. T. N. Pearce, the Essex captain, thus appealed for hit wicket, or possibly bowled. However, the square-leg umpire, Claude Woolley, had been so concerned about the stricken Woodhouse that he did not know exactly what had happened, and umpire McCanlis, at the bowler's end, had been unsighted. Thus Woodhouse was given 'not out', and he went on to make 59 before, more conventionally, getting his leg rather than his head in the way of a straight one.

157

G. W. Hammond reported in 1963 an event which he dated 'some years ago', while on tour in Warwickshire. Hammond was bowling and the ball was played to mid-on, who fielded it and threw it in to the bowler's end. The umpire there ducked to avoid being hit by the throw, but Hammond himself managed to stop the ball and break the wicket with the batsman well out of his crease. The umpire, however, was 'not in a position to give a decision', having taken evasive action a split second earlier. The resourceful Hammond then noticed that the other batsman was well out of his crease too, so he picked up the ball, and threw down the other wicket. Again, a decision was deemed impossible because the square-leg umpire's attention had been diverted by events at the

other end. To complicate matters still further, it was found at the end of all this activity that there were two balls in play, nestling by the stumps at each end. It appeared that the second ball had fallen out of the bowler's umpire's pocket as he ducked, but as both balls were of roughly the same age and condition, it was impossible to tell which was the match ball, and whether the batsman at the striker's end had been 'run out' by the match ball or the other one. Both batsmen remained at the crease, and although Mr Hammond did not record the outcome of the match, I doubt if he bought either of the umpires a drink at close of play.

The Laws of Cricket are sometimes tampered with in the most unsatisfactory way. In 1900, an experiment was conducted at Lord's in which a net, about two feet six inches high, was erected around the boundary, with the idea of making the batsmen run everything out. The idea was dropped after just two first-class matches. In one match a late cut earned the batsman 11 runs, including overthrows.

Before there were any boundaries at all, the wisdom of

the umpires was often brought into play. The *Hampshire Chronicle* reports a match in 1815 in which a ball was struck into one of the many booths which lined what was in effect the playing area. From these booths food and drinks of all types, and occasionally other less honourable services, were sold to the spectators. 'A ball was struck to the booth; a dispute then arose as to the number of runs to be allowed for such a booth-ball. The striker, considering the ball as dead, left his wicket, which was put down. The decision of the umpire was asked, and of the gentleman in the booth, who pronounced him "not out". This caused further dispute, and the match was undecided.'

159

We are now moving into the age of match referees and neutral umpires as gamesmanship takes over from sportsmanship in the professional game. Fortunately for the good of cricket, there are still some top umpires who are happy to be partial when the occasion requires. Standing at John Paul Getty's ground at Wormsley in Oxfordshire in 1992, Test umpire John Holder had to respond to a huge lbw appeal against the Getty XI's opening bat, film star Peter O'Toole. It was the first over of the match, and O'Toole had yet to open his account. 'Not out,' said Holder with conviction. At the end of the over, the square-leg fielder happened to ask Holder how close the decision was. 'Oh, it would have taken all three stumps out of the ground,' replied Holder, with a smile. 'But in a friendly match on a beautiful ground on a sunny afternoon, he's not out until he's off the mark.'

That only goes to show that the umpire is always right.